T3-CAO-730

Novitiate
2 Floor
Textbooks

COPY1

INSIGHTS INTO RELIGIOUS LIFE

INSIGHTS
into
Religious
Life

BY REV. JAMES ALBERIONE, SSP, STD

ST. PAUL EDITIONS

IMPRIMATUR

✛Humberto Cardinal Medeiros
Archbishop of Boston

March 25, 1977

The New American Bible, © 1970, used
herein by permission of the Confraternity
of Christian Doctrine, copyright owner.

Photo credits:

Enit-11
Achilli-43
Quaglini-73
Moisio-79

Library of Congress Cataloging in Publication Data

Alberione, Giacomo Giuseppe, 1884-1971.
   Insights into religious life.

   1. Monastic and religious life.   I. Title.
BX2435.A398   248'.894   77-4862

Copyright, © 1977, by the Daughters of St. Paul

Printed in U.S.A. by the Daughters of St. Paul
50 St. Paul's Ave., Boston, Ma. 02130

The Daughters of St. Paul are an international
religious congregation serving the Church with
the communications media.

FOREWORD

INSIGHTS INTO RELIGIOUS LIFE contains previously unedited lectures of the renowned author and expert on the spiritual life, Very Rev. James Alberione, S.S.P., S.T.D., founder of five Religious Orders and three Secular Institutes.

Offering rich and highly practical reflections, this valuable collection gives attention to fundamental aspects of religious life such as: the call to sanctity, advancement in the spiritual life, the vows, life in the Spirit, life of charity, directions for wise vocational promotion, as well as other important topics pertaining to consecrated life in the service of God.

These thought gems will spark fresh, personal desires to live more intensely the life of dedication to which religious, young and old, have committed themselves.

Spiritual and vocational directors, too, will welcome this little book as a valued aid in their specific apostolate.

Prospective vocations also will find the inspired writings of Father Alberione an enlightening and helpful guide to aid them in making their decision.

CONTENTS

A Lively
Constant and
Predominant
Desire

What is religious profession? It is the profession of love, of perfect love which gives God everything, loving Him with all one's energies, all one's heart, and all one's mind. It is the effort which must be carried out on this earth by men and women religious; it is their specific work, their profession, their activity.

It is a general effort. Every aspect of one's activity and person is to be perfected, so that the mind, will and heart are in God, and Jesus Christ lives in us. If religious work to perfect themselves, they fulfill their mission and respond to their vocation. If, instead, they do not perfect themselves, they do not correspond to their vocation and at the end of their lives, what will they gather up?

What is the principal means of achieving perfection?

The principal means is a real, vivid and profound desire. Desire perfection and will it constantly. The desire for perfection is always under the influence of grace; the desire for sanctity is already thirst for sanctity, for real sanctity, and this thirst comes from God. Therefore, it is a supernatural desire. Such a desire will end only with the attainment of sanctity, but complete sanctity is never achieved, since we will always have imperfections. Yet we must diminish them and reduce their intensity as we gradually move ahead, so that we will no longer hinder the work of Jesus, of the Holy Spirit in us. How many times we stop Him, how many times we give in to little things which serve to satisfy us, but which displease, restrain and put off the work of the Holy Spirit! When we will have passed into eternity, we will see the intimate history of the patient and loving work of God for our sanctification, and we will see if and how we corresponded.

Sanctity is the supreme good of life. There is no other good. Everything else is a means. For the religious, furthermore, it is not only the one and supreme good, but it is also the good which he or she publicly agreed to achieve. Therefore in our profession and in its renewal, let us become ever more aware of this obligation and cultivate it. Let us make the desire for sanctity stronger and stronger within us.

What can you still look for on this earth, you who have given yourself to God? Here is everything: sanctity. So, little by little, as the years go by, continual progress should be evident in religious.

What must be done to have the desire for perfection or sanctity?

Ask it of the Lord; it is a gift of the Holy Spirit. Hence it must be our continual prayer every day to ask the Lord the grace of feeling the desire for perfection more and more. What do I do during the day? What is the good I must procure for myself? This only: greater merit, greater sanctity, greater love of God and neighbor.

This desire must be a trusting one, with the conviction that the Lord will give sanctity to us. It is not meant to torment us as would the desire for something unattainable. Sanctity can be attained by everyone. We, moreover, have a vocation, and it is the vocation to sanctity, that is, to the love of God and of neighbor. This is the thought which should predominate over all others. There are those who desire one thing or another; there are at times preferences for one house or another, for one office or another, for something which our passion seeks, in order to avoid suffering perhaps and so to arrange our life as to suffer less, to work less, to avoid corrections, to live in peace — but in that peace which does not come from the Lord.... A religious may work in the kitchen or teach in a classroom, or do social work; one may enjoy health or suffer sickness, receive pleasant or unpleasant duties.... There will be attachments to the good, to a good which we want.... But one should be attached to God only; to Him alone the whole heart is to be given, the whole mind, the whole will. And God must really predominate over all, over all those worries which we at times go around creating for ourselves, or which come from external things or from our very work. "There is this to be done, that to be done...." There is our sanctity to be achieved first of all!

We cannot say: when I no longer have this burden of ill-health, when they change my duty, when that temptation ceases, when that person who makes me suffer has been changed, when I am a little rested, or when I have again made the annual retreat — then I will start to work. These are temptations! The predominating passion must be sanctity. The predominant thought should be sanctity. Let sanctity be loved and, above all, loved with passion.

The desire for sanctity should also be progressive, constant and not irregular. After having received the sacrament of Penance, some are good for three to four days and then fall again. The same thing happens after retreat: for a week or two all goes well, and then they fall again. The same is true after the spiritual exercises: for a month they are good and then new circumstances come up, fervor begins to diminish, and no more progress is made.

Furthermore, this should be a practical desire, that is, it must lead us to be disposed to suffer anything at all, to fight precisely what impedes progress. When pride enters in, or sentimentality, egoism, or idolatry of one's own body (eating, sleeping, resting and liberty to the extreme limit)...when envies are nourished and grudges are held...then in practice there is no desire for sanctity, because this gives way every time there is a mortification to make, whereas "whoever wishes to come after me, let him deny himself." There is no other law in the Gospel, there is no other way to sanctity. There are two paths in life: one comfortable and the other steep and strewn with thorns and rocks, but this last is the one that leads to heaven.

When one always blames others and never one's self, when one thinks: if we did it this way instead, and why did they dispose things that way...and why do we find ourselves in these circumstances...—these are all excuses to cover up our infidelities, or else to fool ourselves into thinking that we want to become saints, while instead, deep down in our soul, there is no will at all to sanctify ourselves. Then of what use is it? This desire for sanctity must be efficacious — efficacious at any cost, without giving any peace to our ego, and at the same time fulfilling the sacrifices that the day demands of us, thus showing our love of God. Efficacious to what degree? The Theology of Perfection says: even at the cost of health and life. God must be loved more than ourselves; our soul — that is, our sanctification — must be loved more than life itself. If our soul has to suffer some harm because we please ourselves a bit, because we satisfy our selfishness, then we must remedy it. "Deny yourself, take up your cross and follow me" (cf. Lk. 9:23). Each one has his or her own cross, but it is necessary to take it up and carry it constantly.

Efficacious desire! Some would like to put sanctity together with satisfaction, talk a lot about sanctity, of love of God, and point out many ways and many spiritualities.... But the spirituality, the way, is Christ's: "Whoever wishes to be my follower must deny his very self, take up his cross each day, and follow in my steps" (Lk. 9:23).

At times, here and there, ideas and tendencies toward a particular spirituality spring up. These restrict the heart, the spirit.

There is neither this nor that spirituality: there is the Christian spirituality, the spirituality of Jesus Christ: "Deny yourself." Outside these terms there is no way which can lead one to sanctity. It is an illusion to act otherwise. To discuss spirituality a great deal means misunderstanding the Divine Master; it means not having understood what perfection is. What are all these distinctions which, in the end, do not lead to "Christ truly lives in me"? (cf. Gal. 2:20) Let us take the whole Gospel, as it is, as Jesus Christ gave it to us! Let us nourish ourselves on the Gospel and follow its teaching with constancy.

The means for maintaining — in fact, for strengthening — our desire for sanctity are:

■Ask the Lord for it with daily prayer.

■Fortify this desire for sanctity by reflecting that it is our obligation and the work of our whole life, the secret of eternal happiness.

■Struggle against lukewarmness. Lukewarmness hides under many guises and excuses itself with many pretexts.

For progress in perfection careful observance of the constitutions is needed, together with faithfulness to the spirit of the Congregation.

Moreover, in promoting the works of the apostolate and carrying out the duties entrusted to you, be animated by a sincere love of God and of souls, not seeking reward from man but only the reward promised by the Lord to every good work, even the smallest, done for Him or one's neighbor out of love for Him.

Yes, the lively desire, the constant and predominant desire to become a saint is needed. The thought should so predominate that all other preoccupations will have a very remote place. In other words, we must indeed attend to other occupations and carry them out well, but only and always for our sanctification.

Advancing
in
the
Spiritual Life

Prayer is the foundation of the religious life. A religious is one who wants to attain perfection and has chosen the state of perfection. Chastity, poverty, obedience and common life call for abundant energies, but the abundance of graces depends on the abundance of prayer.

Prayer must be ordered chiefly to this — to our own sanctification. We pray for enlightenment of mind, for orientation of the heart toward God and souls, for the fulfillment of God's will — a fulfillment that comprises the observance of the commandments and the religious vows, the practice of virtue and the observance of the Constitutions.

Peace of soul, the joy of a good conscience, the fortune to feel the unity and love of God; the contentment of progressing in perfection; the divine approval of our work, undertakings, study, apostolate; the conviction that God the Father, Jesus Christ, the Holy Spirit, Mary...are with us; the certainty of heaven...these are the fruits of piety.

Our times produce a superficiality and exteriority that easily penetrates religious institutes. Depth is needed in studies, in spiritual work, in formation, in zealous works, in examining our consciences, in all of life.

Today the spirit of laicism has brought about — among other things — a certain disesteem for prayer. Yet action must follow prayer; it cannot precede it. First let us fill ourselves and then give. In the early days of the Church, when the apostles realized that they were so occupied with the work of the apostolate that they could no longer find time for prayer, they chose deacons to help them in their external activities. Thus, they had the renewed possibility of dedicating the necessary time to prayer. Therefore, give importance to prayer, to spiritual work, before all else. Cursed are whatever occupations which would detach us from piety, because we would empty ourselves interiorly and also drain our apostolate.

Who will do the apostolate better and derive greater fruit from it? Eucharistic souls. Jesus in the Eucharist is the Master who teaches us. Jesus in the Eucharist is the Truth, and the eucharistic soul will have greater love for the truth, greater zeal in the apostolate. In fact, the fruit of eucharistic devotion must be love for the apostolate.

The eucharistic soul understands what Jesus' desires are and, with will enkindled, renews the resolution to be diligent in the apostolate.

A privilege, a great gift, the most joyous time of the day is the visit to the Blessed Sacrament. During this time we go to have an audience with Jesus. We meet Him, talk with Him, stay with Him in intimate conversation. For example, one may recall the Samaritan woman, or Nicodemus, or other occasions when Jesus was engaged in such discourses as those we find narrated in St. John's Gospel from the fourteenth chapter onwards. So it is, too, with the sermon on the mount. Out of the twenty-four hours of the day let there surely be this time dedicated to conversation with Jesus Christ!

The practices of piety are to bring about a growth of virtue in us. There is no doubt that sanctity can be reached with them. To those who apply and use them well, the Lord will be generous with comfort, light and consolations. Totally or partially abandoning the practices of piety means closing one's hand to Providence and opening the door to sin, sadness, weariness with the religious life or worse. Instead, to the generosity of the soul will correspond an increasingly merciful generosity of the heavenly Father.

Frequent conversations and a close relationship with Jesus produce friendship, resemblance, identity in thoughts, sentiments and will.

To become one with Jesus Christ — this is a great highway and you can advance on it as far as you wish. Some things are not said in sermons and could not be said, just as some sentiments never emerge from our souls but are reserved only for Jesus. When Jesus has introduced His bride into the private room of His love and of His intimacies, He says mysterious and secret things like those described in the Song of Songs. Follow the doctrine of St. Paul, the first mystic.... You belong to Christ and to Him alone! Enter as deeply as possible into Christ, into His thoughts, into His perfect adoration, into the praise He gives His Father, until you can really say: "Christ lives in me."

Jesus sometimes leads us to the life of union by means of a deep humiliation which forces us to fall to the ground like St. Paul. The great sign of charity is this surrender to everything Jesus wants. This love always has three parts: knowing Jesus better in order to imitate Him, and to love Him more intensely. This life of union with God, this simplified life, is the greatest grace we can receive: we should ask intensely for it, for ourselves and for all those dear to us.

Realizing that a great deal of our effort and time are spent on other things, we must devote some time exclusively to our souls. Thus we understand the invitation of Jesus: "Come by yourselves to an out-of-the-way place and rest a little" (Mk. 6:31). But resting is not the same as sleeping. Rather it is like St. John, the youngest and beloved disciple, resting his head on the adorable bosom of Jesus at the Last Supper. How much did he learn from the beating of that heart! He became the beloved disciple and the disciple of love. This is how we are to rest: rest in God, rest in the heart of God.

We should offer ourselves every day to Jesus, offer ourselves to God as an acceptable victim. Thus our days will be full. Jesus will give Himself directly to us and our life will be meaningful and happy. It is not enough to offer Jesus to the Father: we must also offer ourselves and our work. During His life, Jesus wore Himself out; He offered all His strength to His heavenly Father. We cannot enter paradise without struggle and without the gift of self. Let us walk calmly with our gaze turned to heaven.

Don't be surprised:
"You will weep and mourn
while the world rejoices" (Jn. 16:20).
This means: there will always be mortifica-

tions for those who walk the right road. The practice of virtue and the living of the religious life require a continual sacrifice. But, "your grief will be turned to joy" (Jn. 16:20). Look all the time at your heavenly reward. We are pilgrims on earth. Let us walk on the straight path, not swerving either to the left or the right. The straight path — from the moment we emerged from the waters of Baptism to the moment when we shall say: "It is finished" (cf. Jn. 19:30). And the Lord will receive us in His kingdom and He will say to us as He said to the Good Thief: "This day you will be with me in paradise" (Lk. 23:43). But here on earth we are pilgrims.

Prayer and words alone are not sufficient. We must make some reparation as Christ did. Each one of us simply must be at least slightly mortified. If we have sinned by sight, we should control our eyes. If our tongue has sinned, we should control it. If we have sinned by pride, we should practice humility. Insofar as it depends on us, and keeping in mind our possibilities, we should try to do some service to spread the light of God, the truths which the Lord brought from heaven.

Jesus has won for us the grace to be able to subdue our wills. And so we should say to the Lord: "Not what I want but what You want." We should do this in little things, without anticipating great occasions. Look at Jesus on the cross, with His head bowed in death in submission to the will of His Father.

May God be blessed! How good He is! Men are not like God. Generally, men remember evil more than they remember good. But the Lord is goodness itself. In his letter to the Ephesians, St. Paul stresses very much this thought: that the glory of God lies in the very fact that He showed goodness towards us when He gave us His Son, and that His Son is glorified in giving us His blood, in the redemption. And this means: trust in God, go ahead serenely!

Let all our thoughts be dominated by God; see everything in relation to Him. St. Francis de Sales used to say: "I have only a few desires, and if I could be born again, I would have only one—God." This is simplicity. The person who truly seeks God in everything achieves a life of union with Him.

The
Real
Holocaust

It is important to have a clear understanding of the true meaning of obedience. Prior to the vow of obedience, we have the fourth commandment, which establishes the obligation to obey both parents and superiors.

The spirit of obedience presupposes a meek, well-balanced, docile character, a natural or acquired respect for superiors, and sufficient intellectual capacity to understand the religious vow of obedience.

What is obedience? The word "obedience" comes from the Latin, *ob audio,* meaning to listen: one heeds authority when it speaks....

To heed because the superior is good is not obedience. To heed because we like the command is not obedience. To heed because the superior allows us to do what we want is not obedience. *Obedience consists in heeding because of the authority of God.* This is liberating obedience. One can obey even the most unattractive people, as did Jesus. He obeyed His crucifiers, Pilate, and Herod, because through these men, who were neither wise nor good, He received God's dispositions. In fact, "there is no authority except from God" (Rom. 13:1).

Religious obedience is the submission of our will to God's not in a vague, general way, but *as specified by our Rule.*

Ordinarily, during the day obedience is identified with community life, and we live community life when we perform daily duties well.

Obedience entails observing the Rule, carrying out the duty assigned, being punctual in keeping the schedule, submitting to the confessor, to moral and spiritual direction and adapting to what God disposes in our regard.

Obedience is the observance of the commandments and the practice of common life concerning food, lodging, etc.

Obedience means giving ourselves entirely to God, offering ourselves in homage to God, saying: "I am Your servant; speak and I will listen. Just make Your desire known to me. I do not expect You to command me according to my liking. Do with me what You will. I only want to follow Your wishes."

Obedience means giving up doing everything as we would choose, even in such things as choice of practices of piety or acts of penance.

Obedience is a moral virtue and when the vow is added to it, it becomes a great means of sanctification, a powerful way to attain the perfection of the saints, which consists in seeking only the glory of God and striving for perfection in order to glorify God.

The only sure sanctity is conformity of one's will to God's. And this conformity must prove itself by the exact, constant fulfillment of the divine will. Hence, because of the vow of obedience, religious life is the most suitable, easiest and safest road to sanctity.

Obedience is *the first and principal virtue of religious life.* The other two virtues of chastity and poverty, which also are vows, are observed if one observes obedience. In fact, it is important to give God our body and all we own for His service, but to give Him our will is a much more valuable gift. It is the principal homage to offer our Lord.

There is nothing better in heaven or on earth than always to say "yes" to God. By giving Him our will, we give Him "the best part."

Obedience is a difficult virtue and certainly requires many sacrifices, but it is the virtue *that prepares for us the greatest reward* because it includes humility and faith—the humility of submission and the faith that is pleasing to God.

Obedience is *central to religious life....* It is the real holocaust of those who make the vows and observe them. It is a holocaust offered to God, an act of adoration by which we acknowledge God as Lord and Master of all, absolutely perfect, supreme Authority, and we admit that we are lowly creatures.... We acknowledge all this and adore His will. Our entire day is spent in adoration, no matter what we are doing.

Obedience *offers a complete homage to God,* the most perfect love. *It is the cult of latria,* which consists in adoring God as the infinite, supreme Authority, the first and highest Good, the supreme Lord and Creator, whose dominion over us is without limit. Obedience, therefore, is praise of God's wisdom, acknowledging that His wisdom is good, His power is infinite and His rule is over all.

Obedience is precious because it *confers security.* When we carry out a directive, we feel tranquil. When, instead, we do as we please, we cannot be certain of having rightly interpreted God's desires, and we experience doubt.

Obedience *brings peace and serenity.* Doing our own will brings uneasiness.

When we are obedient, we enjoy *great freedom,* since we submit to God alone and to those who represent Him. Thus we are neither ruled by our egoism nor by impressions, but by God, our Creator and Father.

He who obeys, permitting himself to be ruled by God, *rules the world*. He becomes the master of everything — he is free and in full control of his passions, his carnal instincts, his pride and his vanity. He is the ruler because he gives everything to God. "And the truth will set you free" (Jn. 8:32). The individual who obeys grows strong. As Cicero used to say, "We are slaves to the law in order to become free."

The obedient become rulers because they are powerful with God. In fact, God does the will of those who obey Him.

If a person places himself entirely in the hands of God and of those whom He uses, he will do all the good expected of him by God, thus corresponding fully to the Lord's plans in his regard.

God destines us for various things. If we accept what He disposes for us, He will not abandon us. With the sacrifices we must make He sends us His grace. Moreover, what great comfort, consolation and confidence we enjoy when we work for God!

Obedience gives us *the certainty that our life is pleasing to God.* . . . When we obey, we please God. Contrariwise, when our actions or undertakings do not proceed from obedience but are only ours, they manifest our personal will, even if we hide them under the pretext of a desire to do better or more.

Obedience *gives us the certainty of being on the path of sanctity*. It assures us that we are doing the will of God to the end of our lives — when we will submit to death as we have been submissive throughout life. This is an easy way to become saints.

Obedience gives us *the assurance of receiving the grace to carry out the duties assigned us*. When God wants us to do a particular thing, He grants us the grace to do it. Thus, if we strive to observe our Constitutions, we truly receive the grace to observe them. However, when one chooses on his own to do something, he is left alone to do it. And success is in direct proportion to the obedience in which an act is performed, because of the factor of God's grace. Also, we enjoy peace, because we are not plagued with worries and anxiety about our actions.

If we wash or sweep in the spirit of obedience, we acquire more merits than if we do something "more important" on our own.

Perfect obedience brings us *to the highest degree of love of God*, and will make us happy in the life to come. Our happiness, in fact, will consist in glorifying God. And if our soul prepares itself by always striving for God's greater honor and glory, after death it will immediately be led into eternal glory.

The Lord rewards only what is done for Him alone. He tells us that on the day of judgment, to those who complain that they merited more because "in Your name we prophesied...," He will say, "Be gone. You did what you wanted." God will not even reward penance or practices of piety that were of our own choosing, and were not His will. That is why the saints did their utmost to avoid anything which savored of their own choosing, even in apostolic zeal. They also accepted spiritual direction to be certain of gaining the merit of obedience.

Obedience is the best way *to express love for one's Congregation*, and as long as the spirit of obedience is maintained, a great peace will permeate the entire Congregation.

It is very important to preserve the spirit of and to conform to one's own Congregation. For this purpose, union of mind, heart and will is to be fostered.

What is needed is a tendency to interpret events well, to judge directives in a positive way, and to love the Congregation for its Rules, its apostolate, its means of achieving sanctity. Obedience comes easier to those who love their Congregation; they are inclined to see good in it, and in whatever function they fulfill, they feel themselves to be playing an important role in the Congregation.

Naturally, not everyone can be on the same level. Nor is this even desirable, for the one who best performs the will of God earns the most merit. Of the various tasks, one may be better than another, but the merit depends on the love with which the tasks are performed.

Some individuals are excitable and speedy by nature, while others are calmer and slower. This situation is an occasion for greater merit: let the one who is always in a rush slow down a bit, and let the one lagging behind try to move faster. Both will thus be doing the will of God in this situation.

Obedience preserves harmony and union in a community. A Congregation offers many means to achieve its goal, but how are these means to be fused and channeled toward it? Obedience is the answer, for it keeps the order needed. What would happen in a community if there were as many hours of rising in the morning as there are members? But if all make the small sacrifice of rising at the same time, the situation changes.

A community that lacks order and harmony—the results of obedience—becomes lax and annoyed with itself. Naturally, if someone needs it, an exception should be made without hesitation. But exceptions must not become the rule, or unity will disappear.

Jesus
Model of
Obedience

There can be no sanctification without imitation of Jesus, who was submissive to His Father's will even to the point of death, and death on the cross.

Jesus gave us the most perfect example of obedience. The Gospel relates: *"He was obedient to them"* (Lk. 2:51). He, the Son of God Incarnate and infinite wisdom, was subject to two of His creatures. Thus He did everything His Father wanted, in His private and public life, and on to the acceptance of the bitter chalice in the Garden of Gethsemane with the words: "Not my will but yours be done" (Lk. 22:42).

Jesus walked the road of obedience. We might think that He should have done His own will and been His own guide. In fact, He could not have made any mistakes, because He did not have corrupt passions as we do. Neither could He have been deceived, since He is Truth Itself, the Wisdom of the Father.

Yet Jesus willed to obey. Through the will of the Father He became man, was born poor in Bethlehem, fled to Egypt, and later returned to Nazareth, to grow up in that humble house. The evangelist summarizes His private life thus: *He was obedient to them.* Jesus was subject to Joseph and Mary.

Even as an adult, He continued the complete, total submission He had practiced as a child. He obeyed down to the smallest detail, keeping to the schedule for prayer, work, meals, rest — everything. These decisions were made by Joseph and Mary, and Jesus obeyed.

In the Garden of Gethsemane, when He was about to begin His passion, Jesus' prayer was one of complete submission to the Father: "My Father, if this cup cannot pass away unless I drink it, your will be done." Christ's obedience during the passion extended even to His crucifiers. While insults were being heaped on Him, He permitted Himself to be crucified without uttering a complaint, as an innocent lamb led to the slaughter. Throughout the passion, Jesus was totally submissive to His Father's will. Not one act of His showed an unwilling acceptance of it; on the contrary, He did it serenely to the very end. Jesus is the great Teacher of obedience.

When He obeyed Joseph, it certainly was not because of the latter's superior wisdom. The motive for Christ's obedience was His foster-father's *authority,* since by the will of God, Joseph represented the heavenly Father. Hence, what Jesus said regarding His Father, He could also have said concerning St. Joseph: "I always do what pleases him" (Jn. 8:29). For Jesus carried out God's dispositions as He received them through Joseph.

From Bethlehem's manger to Calvary, Christ's whole life was one of continuous, diligent, perfect obedience. He had begun His life by descending into Mary's womb out of obedience—"he became flesh" (Jn. 1:14)—and He continued to obey until death: "He humbled himself, obediently accepting even death, death on a cross" (Phil. 2:8). Of His life, the Gospel says: "He came to Nazareth and was obedient to them" (Lk. 2:51). He was submissive for thirty years! What greater example could we ask for!

It is hard to decide which marvel is greater—two creatures giving orders to God, or the virtue which renders this God obedient to two creatures!

Later, during His public life, in obedience to the Father, Jesus performed many miracles, suffered numerous humiliations, underwent hunger, thirst and weariness, slept on the ground under a tree or sought lodging here and there—always disposed to do the will of His Father. And He put up with Judas, who was plotting against Him and even stealing their alms.

The Father was well pleased with every moment of Jesus' life, right to the end. "I always do what is pleasing to the Father" (cf. Jn. 8:29). Three times in the Garden of Gethsemane He repeated: "My Father, if this cannot pass me by without my drinking it, your will be done" (Mt. 26:42). Then He went to meet His enemies saying: "This is your hour" (Lk. 22:53). Obediently He bowed His head when condemned by Annas, Caiaphas and Pilate, and accepted the cross His Father had assigned to Him. Obediently He carried it and in the same spirit stretched Himself on it. There He remained for the exact number of hours and minutes willed by the Father—without trying to shorten or prolong the time. Finally, at the end He was able to say: "Now it is finished" (Jn. 19:30). All that His Father willed had been fulfilled. With that He bowed His head, and delivered over His spirit (cf. Jn. 19:30).

Jesus was always thinking of His Father and working for Him. Everything He did was for His Father's glory. He lived in His presence uninterruptedly. For this reason the Father attested of Him: "You are my beloved Son. On you my favor rests" (Lk. 3:22).

May He be able to look upon us too with pleasure at our imitation of His Son's heroic obedience.

Good
Community
Living

We live in a society: we are members of a civil society, of a religious society, of a congregation. Living in a society entails specific obligations towards our fellow members, because we are in continual contact with them and we influence them either for good or for evil. No one can say: "Well, perhaps I do not give good example, but at least I am not a cause of scandal." It cannot be so. Our conduct leaves an impression on others.

Simply doing nothing is already a source of disedification. because we have to do good. Tepidity or mediocrity is already a shortcoming in this regard, because we are obliged to edify others and not influence them to be lukewarm themselves. We cannot say: "I mind my own business." If only this were true—that everyone minded his own business!

St. Bernard said to Pope Eugene III: "To yourself be first, to yourself be last." In other words, let your first thoughts and worries be about your life, similarly also your last thoughts. Let your every concern begin from yourself.

Notwithstanding what the Saint said, we are always leaving an impression on others. Even if we go on saying: "I mind my own business," we are a source of edification or disedification.

It is very important that we examine our attitude in our relations with others. The good, mature person who is capable of adapting himself to others is a powerful apostolic force, while the contrary is one of the greatest impediments to good. The person of character is he who possesses strong convictions and endeavors firmly and consistently to conform his life to them.

A pleasant disposition implies the blending of goodness and firmness, of charm and strength, of frankness and tact, thus deserving the love and esteem of those with whom we deal. The ill-natured person, instead, is rude in his manners and allows his egoism to dominate him. He is disagreeable and lacks goodness and delicacy.

There should be joy in our houses. The house should be an oasis where physical needs find relief. It should be outstanding for the peace and harmony reigning therein. All of us have some sharp angles in our character, some unpleasant traits...but we should live like people who love one another. "Love is patient; love is kind" (1 Cor. 13:4).

Good humor is an added help. We can't live in perpetual tension. Banish the gloomy faces. Our apostolate in itself is exacting. Our houses, therefore, should favor joyful relaxation. We should be patient but we must not try the patience of others.

In community life we are sometimes a burden to one another. There are those who have worked and have exhausted all their strength, perhaps in silence and obscurity, and are sometimes not even appreciated. Rather, they are treated badly or even despised. Those who have reached a high degree of self-sacrifice are able to bear these things joyfully. However, it must also be said that people who cause such suffering and are blind to the virtues of others commit an act of injustice. And yet, there are, and there always will be, these trials in religious communities.

Let us not deceive ourselves. We are not living with perfect people and we are not perfect either. The best among us are those who are striving for perfection. "Help carry one another's burdens" (Gal. 6:2). However, those who realize that they are a burden should reflect on their serious responsibility before God and should amend their ways.

In small houses, particularly, life is sometimes reduced to a real purgatory, where some are not able to hold out and just give up under the strain.

Sometimes a person burns with envy, and the consequences are divisions and discontent. Envy is a passion that blinds and hardens the heart. Humility, instead, inspires kind words, charitable sentiments, good wishes for others. It renders a person available to the needs of others. Let the gentle figure of the Divine Master be ever before us and let us keep His words in mind: "Learn from me, for I am gentle and humble of heart" (Mt. 11:29).

Are there occasional mistakes? If there are, let's practice Jesus' teaching in this regard: "Go and point out his fault, but keep it between the two of you.... If he does not listen, summon another, so that every case may stand on the word of two or three witnesses. If he ignores them, refer it to the church" (Mt. 18:15-17). The Congregation is a society, a religious family.

Some are able to discover the good all the time! They take note of the smallest favor received and they are quick to forget any wrong done them. Those who continually see what is wrong and always have something of which to accuse others or rebuke them are not goodhearted. Sometimes it takes only a smile to settle many things.

Good relations with our fellow members is of prime importance. St. Paul says: "Make my joy complete by your unanimity, possessing the one love, united in spirit and ideals. Never act out of rivalry or conceit; rather, let all parties think humbly of others as superior to themselves, each of you looking to others' interests rather than his own" (Phil. 2:2-4).

Again, he says: "I plead with you, then… to live a life worthy of the calling you have received, with perfect humility, meekness and patience, bearing with one another lovingly. Make every effort to preserve the unity which has the Spirit as its origin and peace as its binding force. There is but one Body and one Spirit, just as there is but one hope given all of you by your call" (Eph. 4:1-4).

Let us also ask for the grace to understand rightly the doctrine of the Mystical Body. We are members of the Mystical Body. If one member is healthy, all the members feel his beneficial influence. A healthy member has a large sphere of influence on the others, even if he does not know them or they are far away from him. Moreover, he draws down graces for the Church, the Pope, and the faithful.

In community life, the different parts form one whole. St. Paul explains this by an example: "If the body were all eye, what would happen to our hearing?" (1 Cor. 12:17) Similarly, a certain variety is called for in common life: there must be integral unity but a diversity of functions.

In a house, the entire edifice is a house but there are different stories and rooms. Jesus said: "I am the vine..." (Jn. 15:5), but the roots, the branches and the leaves are also parts, indeed, necessary parts of the vine. The same is true of common life.

Evidently, there is diversity among the members of a religious congregation, but diversity in unity. Union is found in the joining of spirits, in the Holy Spirit. In other words, there must be the grace of the Holy Spirit, the love of Jesus, the bond of charity uniting all hearts into one, in everything.

The practice of community life, which is a great means of holiness, is included in our profession. Community life consists of shared thoughts and aspirations, not however to the exclusion of diversity. There ought to be a union of strength.

Community life is a life lived under obedience. It is the harmonious living together of the brethren. It means putting together every effort for sanctification and for the apostolate. We are not concerned only with our own sanctification but also with the salvation of others.

We must make a gift of ourselves to the Church. We must feel that we are members of the Mystical Body, living and working in the Church. This is a continuous exercise of charity in action. "The love of Christ has gathered us together."

A
Lifetime
of
Service

Jesus gave Himself for our Redemption. Through our zeal we have to help Him to save men and bring the Redemption to completion.

May our apostolate sound powerfully the call to resurrection: "It is now the hour for you to wake from sleep" (Rom. 13:11). "O men, rise and begin to detest what you have followed; begin to follow Christ whom you have ignored and despised!"

Religious life has had its ups and downs in the course of centuries. It has swayed slightly to the right and slightly to the left, like a pendulum. But it must do as Jesus did: blend the interior life and the apostolate.

Down through the centuries, this is what happened: at first, the slogan was "Flee, flee!" The advice given then was to flee from the world and take refuge in solitude. But there came a moment when others said: "Why retire into solitude? No! Let's go to the people; let's work and preach!" And this was the other extreme. Keep in the middle of the road as Jesus and Mary did: holiness and apostolate together!

Whoever wants to lead people to ideals of holiness and of eternity must be poor in spirit. The person who wishes to lead them to purity of life must be chastely virginal. Anybody who desires to inspire people to lead a Christian family life, and to have order in society, in the unity of the Church, must be obedient.

Let us give what will purify and elevate people more, not what is most sought after by men. "If I were trying to win man's approval, I would surely not be serving Christ!" (Gal. 1:10) Even among the faithful, we find those who look for what is less useful, less perfect. The wise and holy apostle gives and endeavors to make acceptable what is more useful for eternity. We need the Christian outlook; we need to develop Christian thought within ourselves, and then zealously share it. We endeavor to teach the Faith especially to the poorer classes, to those who are infants in matters of faith and still more to those who have no faith and no prayer life.

What would St. Paul, wholly fired by the love of God, do now? "Who will separate me from the love of Christ? Even if we are troubled or worried, or being persecuted, or lacking food or clothes, or being threatened or even attacked – nothing can come between us and the love of Christ" (cf. Rom. 8:35). Nothing! So what did he do? He traversed the world preaching and sanctifying every-one who came near him, inspiring all by his example and holy life. Sensitive to the universality of his mission, he spread the fragrance of Christ...in many nations.

The love of God abounds in us to the point of our wanting Him to be known and loved. "His kingdom come." What the soul needs is the fire of two flames: the love of God and the love of others. In love there is life. "The charity of Christ urges me on."

The apostolate is an endless profession of charity; it is the dedication of one's entire life to people. It calls for sacrifice. We should either not undertake it at all, or embrace generously the sacrifices it demands. Under-take the apostolate in a supernatural spirit. Undertake it as it is. Accept whatever awaits us, even if we see that we must try to progress through a world comparable to a forest. We have to make our way painfully and cou-rageously.

At the end of St. Paul's various missions, the conclusion for him was almost always... persecutions, calumnies, beatings.

We will overspend ourselves to educate young people who will forget the benefits received and will rebuke us for our old-fashioned methods and for the way we taught them. Our service, full of dedication and sacrifice, will be met by the blackest ingratitude, if not indeed by accusations. We will spend long hours in apostolic work, and have a totally disappointing result. We will show the utmost love, only to see that the more we love, the less are we loved. We work hard to serve many people and in old age we may be just barely tolerated. Paul, in his last letter from the Roman prison (his second imprisonment), writes as follows to Timothy: "Do your best to join me soon, for Demas, enamored of the present world, has left me.... Alexander the coppersmith did me a great deal of harm.... At the first hearing of my case in court no one took my part..." (2 Tm. 4:9-16). But what was St. Paul's reaction to this? "I am overflowing with joy in the midst of all my tribulations."

The apostolate has its own fatigue, discouragement and disappointments. There are those who don't understand this. But was Jesus' apostolate understood by all? 'Think of Him. The city of Samaria closed its doors and the apostles asked that fire descend on it. Jesus, however, did not come to castigate or put the city to flame. Rather He came to inflame our hearts with His love.

If your Congregation, or better still, your religious family, felt its obligation of charity towards all, and tried through the apostolate to pay its debt to men and to God, then you would have the perfection of charity and consequently of holiness. There is one thing which helps a great deal: the practice of charity inside the Congregation in general, and in each house in particular.

A
Lifetime
of
Fidelity

In our Lord's various prophecies about His death, His conclusion was always: "And on the third day I will rise again" (cf. Mk. 9:31). And He did rise on the third day. This will also happen to us.

The resurrection of Jesus Christ must make us think of our resurrection. When Jesus went to the grave of Lazarus, Martha said to Him: "'Lord, if you had been here, my brother would never have died. Even now, I am sure that God will give you whatever you ask of him.'

"'Your brother will rise again,' Jesus assured her.

"'I know he will rise again,' Martha replied, 'in the resurrection on the last day.' Jesus told her:

'I am the resurrection and the life: whoever believes in me,
though he should die, will come to life; and whoever is alive and believes in me will never die.
Do you believe this?'

"'Yes, Lord,' she replied. 'I have come to believe that you are the Messiah, the Son of God: he who is to come into the world'" (Jn. 11:21-28).

Here, then, are the two resurrections: Christ's, which occurred on the third day, and ours, which will take place at the end of the world.

Jesus was calumniated, beaten, scourged and crowned with thorns. He was dragged from one tribunal to another. He was condemned as one unworthy to live because He had said the truth. He had defended His divine kingship; He had sought the glory of the Father and He had announced that one day He would come to judge all men. He was condemned to death and crucified. Such was the death of the Savior of the world. But His holy body was not to remain in the sepulcher. Reduced to a state similar to a crushed worm, it was not to remain thus. God would glorify it. And all that He had suffered was changed into a reason for joy.

So will it be with us. Every hardship, every mortification that we endure now, will one day be turned into glory. Every act of self-denial will be our glory.

Religious profession means sacrifice, an offering: I belong to God. God can use me in whatever way He wants. I have no will of my own. I have offered everything to Him and thus I immolate myself for the Lord a little every day. We should offer God our gradually declining health and our time, accepting whatever the Lord may decree for us and devoting ourselves to good works, to works which are holy because they are done for Him. Let us offer our sacrifice.

Truly, the human heart has never known, and will never know on earth the consolation, the joys and the bliss which God has prepared for those who love Him, as St. Paul said.

Blessed are those who were wise enough to spend all their energy for God! Blessed is the good religious, the religious faithful to the end! That heart and that being wholly spent for Jesus Christ will be completely satisfied. No desire, no power of the body or soul will remain unfulfilled. The joys we love to imagine but which Jesus has kept partially hidden from us so that we may exercise faith—these will be ours forever.

Do we truly employ all our strength for Jesus Christ? Blessed are those who, after a day spent for the Lord, can say at night: "I am really tired and feel the need for rest." If they take rest, it is only to reawaken to more fervent service of the Lord, to greater diligence and hard work in their apostolate, so that it will do more and more good.

At the end of our life we will be weary from the long journey of life—for some it will be longer, for others, shorter—but when life's voyage has been made with the Lord, it is always a happy one. And it is a journey that will be crowned by eternal repose.

In the presence of the death of certain people, we feel inclined to bow our heads in reverence. Looking upon their bodies, we think of Jesus' words to Martha: "Your brother will rise" (Jn. 11:23). And we are consoled.

Jesus Christ, our Lord and our Pasch, has been sacrificed. The resurrection of Christ is the forerunner and the source of grace for our resurrection. It represents our own resurrection. Jesus comes out of the sepulcher, and we must come out of the tomb of sins and defects. Jesus comes out of the sepulcher and will no longer remain in that tomb of death. We must come out of the sepulcher and no longer go into those occasions which make us fall, occasions which are dangerous because they lead to sin.

Jesus leaves the sepulcher, never again to enter it, to remind us that the resolutions we make now should be lasting ones. We have risen in Christ "in our minds" and this means that we must have new thoughts, we must have yearnings for heaven, for eternity, for that day when the angel will give everyone the signal to rise. We shall rise with a glorious body if our body has been made holy by work, by prayer, by virtue, and by the service of God.

Live

in

Joy

Joy comes from God: God is beatitude itself, and those who carry God in their heart participate in this joy. Certainly they cannot reach perfect happiness on this earth, but they can possess that peace which is possible here.

Let everyone try to eliminate the sadness, melancholy and nervousness which would weigh heavily on fellow religious as well as on oneself. The causes of this dejection could be sin, scruples, the habit of viewing things suspiciously or of interpreting everything negatively, of expecting one trouble after another, of completely surrendering to impressions and becoming overly affected by sad events.

Has sin been committed? Confession restores peace and tranquillity. Are there scruples? Obedience to the confessor will cure them. Is there the habit of always looking at the dark side of things? A firm resolution to distrust one's judgment should straighten out this situation. The habit of always interpreting and judging well is extremely necessary in community life.

The devil's greatest efforts are directed toward making souls the prey of discouragement and distrust. He must be fought by looking for reasons and motives for encouragement and trust.

It is true that in religious life many sacrifices are to be made. But a religious who is aware of making them for Jesus, of living with Him, of being helped by Mary, will always sacrifice with a joyful face and a smile. "Rejoice in the Lord always! I say it again. Rejoice!" said St. Paul (Phil. 4:4).

We religious should strive for both individual and communitarian happiness. May every house have members who bring a ray of holy joy. This serenity will contribute to the health and peace of all the members of the community. It will also ease the tension and fatigue during moments of trial and sorrow.

May holy joy always permeate our religious family. Prayer will improve, and it will be easier to overlook many "molehills" which, when seen through sad eyes, become "mountains."

It is up to religious to convince the world that those who live in the house of God are happy because they possess the grace of God. Their smiling faces will reveal a joyful heart to everyone, showing that they are happy to be of service and to do good. Joy shines out and makes a good, beneficial impression. So let there be joyful souls, joyful communities, joyful apostolic labor. Happy people reach sanctity faster.

True, there are occasions for tears. Nevertheless, sadness will not solve a problem....

Another way that leads to happiness is the right intention:

"Glory to God in high heaven,
  peace on earth to those on whom his favor
    rests" (Lk. 2:14).

When a soul has achieved a holy detachment in every regard, to both the pleasant and the unpleasant, and wants every action to be a fragrant offering to God, he or she is off to a good start. There will be a readiness to do God's will and to begin each day leaning on Christ for support.

It is God who fills us with joy and lets us experience the truth that He Himself is our reward "exceedingly great."

With reason St. Paul exclaimed: "I am filled with consolation, and despite my afflictions my joy knows no bounds" (2 Cor. 7:4). When he and Barnabas were imprisoned, the jailers were stunned to hear their voices rising in song from the lower dungeons. St. Paul knew well that the fullest days are those marked by the cross!

It is true that the heart can really suffer and at times feel the need to say with Jesus: "Father, if it is possible, let this cup pass me by," but then immediately we add: "Let it be as you would have it, not as I" (Mt. 26:39).

The soul is certain that our heavenly Father loves her, looks upon her approvingly, and awaits her in His blessed kingdom. He will seat her at His table and will quench her thirst with His chalice of eternal joy.

Let us therefore carefully preserve the right intention. The right intention gives courage when things go wrong, when we are tired, when we are misunderstood. It does much to draw God's blessings upon us.

At times we may make mistakes. We may sow but not reap. It matters not. We shall reap tomorrow — or others will. And the merit belongs to those who work, not to those who reap.

Let us therefore live in holy joy and have the right intentions. The Lord will do the rest.

When we walk beneath Mary's mantle, nourish ourselves on the Word of God and the Eucharist, and keep our eyes on heaven, what more could we want? Only heaven — and that will be our overwhelming, never-ending joy.

Let Us
Work
for
Heaven!

Jesus Christ rose from the dead, ascended into heaven, and sits at the right hand of the Father. He will come to judge all men, and proclaim the final destiny of the good: "Come. You have my Father's blessing! Inherit the kingdom prepared for you from the creation of the world" (Mt. 25:34).

Why do men eagerly seek the things of earth? Why do they not remember that there is a heaven? They forget the great joys God has prepared for the good. Therefore, sins, concessions to the flesh, unbridled ambition and attachment to the things of the earth follow. They look for happiness here below, instead of looking for it elsewhere.

Everyone should think of heaven, but religious in particular. Many regrets and problems would then disappear. When a religious pronounces the vows, he says to the Lord: "I do not want anything else on this earth, Lord, only You, only heaven." The more a religious raises his thoughts to heaven, the more he is fervent, virtuous and zealous. How can good vocations be recruited if they are not shown the great advantage of religious life? A person will gladly give his life, his all, if he knows he can gain the "All" — the Lord!

When thinking of heaven, let us keep three things in mind:

— Reflect that paradise will be the vision, the possession and the enjoyment of God; meditate on the fact that our heart will be filled with joy only in heaven — indeed we will overflow with happiness — for only God is infinite.

Certain conversations of religious sound like what one would expect from non-believers! They believe in heaven (they say so when they recite the Creed), but then they live as though heaven did not exist.... Their concern is to secure for themselves little earthly pleasures and comforts.

— Orient our life towards heaven. As good businessmen, let us think of the reward which awaits us, of the end for which we were created, and then direct our whole lives toward it. Let us reflect on the "hundred-fold" promised to those who make the required renunciations.

— Pray to obtain an increase of faith in heaven. "I believe, O Lord, but increase my faith in paradise." Faith is a gift of God! There are two great truths not only to be believed, but also to "feel": that there is a God by whom we were created and to whom we must return, and that this God rewards good and punishes evil. He will reward us! When we labor for Him, therefore, we are really working for our own interests.

Why is it that at times we go about our work so slowly? Because we do not think of the great reward we can obtain by using to its utmost every moment of our life. The religious who frequently thinks of heaven will always be stable, constant and fervent.

Contrariwise, the religious whose faith in heaven is weak, and who seldom thinks of it will have little fervor and zeal. And even if he works a great deal, he will not be sure of reaping the fruits of his labor, for he can be compared to those businessmen who work very hard, but earn very little for heaven. It is not what one does that counts, but the right intention with which it is done. Oh how wise is the good religious!

Let us ask the Lord for this wisdom. The religious life is based on this thought: "Everyone who has given up home, brothers or sisters, father or mother, wife or children or property for my sake, will receive many times as much and inherit everlasting life" (Mt. 19:29).

After having been taken up into heaven to contemplate its beauty, St. Paul said: "I long to be freed from this life and to be with Christ" (Phil. 1:23). Let us think of heaven and rejoice! *I am working for heaven!* I am not struggling for a hope which will disappoint me. I am working, awaiting the blessed hope and coming of our Lord Jesus Christ.

Let us exercise the virtue of hope more intensely. In times of difficulty and temptation, think of heaven. The religious who keeps his eyes on the goal hastens his steps and does not feel weary. Or, even if he does feel tired, he loves the very weariness itself, and is courageous and fervent. He finds new ways of working for his sanctification and for the apostolate.

Remember heaven, therefore, particularly at the outset of the day. As soon as we awaken, let our thought be: "Today I shall work for heaven!"

The
Holy Spirit
Gives Us
Jesus

Together with the apostles, Mary made the first novena to the Holy Spirit. And what a great one it was! The Blessed Virgin who, alone in her little home at Nazareth, had once implored the heavenly Father to send His divine Son, and who hastened the coming of Jesus, the Redeemer, now continued to implore and once again obtained the descent of the Holy Spirit with all His gifts. Mary already knew the Holy Spirit: He had descended on her and had caused the Son of God to take flesh. You see who gives Jesus — the Holy Spirit!

The Holy Spirit is the Love of the Father and the Son; He will make you think, work and speak according to the Faith. The Holy Spirit has to bring about a higher type of prayer in you, a more elevated and deeply-felt spirit of prayer, a more serene and unruffled dedication to the will of God and to your Congregation, a way of working in the apostolate totally in harmony with the Spirit of Christ. Have God as your goal, count on God and work for God: "Apart from me you can do nothing..." (Jn. 15:5). "In him who is the source of my strength I have strength for everything" (Phil. 4:13).

If you want to reach the highest degree of your vocation, its most sublime peak, you need a great and continuous infusion of the Holy Spirit. Love for divine things, detachment from the world, love for the evangelical counsels — all this is a divine gift. Everything in us should be the work of the Holy Spirit: "begotten not by blood, nor by carnal desire, nor by man's willing it, but by God" (Jn. 1:12). No, it is not from the will of man but from God that, like Jesus Christ, we are born through the work of the Holy Spirit.

The Holy Spirit is power. He gives inspirations, instills love, communicates generosity. Daily meditation will be of immense profit if we place ourselves under the light of the Holy Spirit, as the apostles, the holy women and the disciples did when they were gathered together in the Cenacle on the morning of Pentecost.

The apostles began to preach when they had been filled with the Holy Spirit. We should do the same: first fill ourselves with the Holy Spirit — that is, with heavenly wisdom, grace, love of God, virtue — and then give what we possess. Give heavenly wisdom through the apostolate. Give virtue through good example. Give — that is, obtain — grace through prayer, particularly eucharistic and liturgical prayer. Let our first commitment be that of nourishing ourselves, not that of giving. To give words not accompanied by grace is to beat the air or pound a drum that makes noise but gives no life. If, instead, our words proceed from the Holy Spirit, living in us, they will become spirit and life.

I think that often there is need for a great infusion of the gifts of the Holy Spirit, because certain people find the life of prayer difficult. But the gifts of the Holy Spirit are in us in the measure in which we make room for them in our souls. If these gifts flourish later on because we have corresponded to them, then virtue will become much easier for us; it will be more perfectly exercised and will even bring a certain consolation, a sort of joy and interior peace. This will be the fruit of the indwelling of the Holy Spirit in us.

If we would only try to reinforce our devotion more, and to stir up in ourselves faith in the work of the Holy Spirit! We would thus be walking on the right path. He will be the Master; we will be His true disciples, allowing ourselves to be attracted and guided not by passion but by the clear light and grace of the Holy Spirit: "All who are led by the Spirit of God are sons of God" (Rom. 8:14). Let us look at our devotion to the Holy Spirit, the great Unknown One, who is often considered an outsider by men, while He is truly the One who makes everyone holy!

Directed
by
the
Holy Spirit

The gifts of the Holy Spirit are seven supernatural habits which vigorously urge us to do good and to fulfill our commitments, spurring us on towards holiness. They render easier what is naturally very difficult.

When the Holy Spirit comes, He re-creates a new life in a soul. And if He infuses His gifts more fully, then we walk with a cheerful and generous heart in the way of holiness, almost not feeling any burden, although burdens and trials always accompany us.

The gifts of *knowledge and understanding* enlighten us, casting a vibrant, penetrating and extraordinary light on revealed truths and giving us the true meaning of God's Word. Jesus has told us: "I am the light of the world" (Jn. 8:12). With veneration and humility let us hear this from His lips, together with what He adds: "You are the light of the world" (Mt. 5:14). Jesus is the light, and we are to be reflectors, receiving it and reflecting it to mankind.

The gifts of knowledge and understanding impart a supernatural light to us. By way of example, we can say: Were we created for God? Then we must direct our life towards Him. Were we created for heaven? Then we must direct our life towards heaven; we want to take the narrow way which leads to God.

Sometimes a person may become indifferent. The soul in the state of indifference is indeed in a very distressing and dangerous state. Every kind of evil, even the worst, can result from indifference.

We are to ask, therefore, for the gifts of knowledge and understanding in order to shape our lives according to faith.

The gift of *counsel* is the lamp of the Holy Spirit. With it the practical intelligence sees and directs what has to be done in particular cases, as well as the means to be used. The Scriptures give us a maxim to remember: My son, "do nothing without counsel and then you need have no regrets" (Sir. 32:19).

A serious error especially in vogue today is the spirit of independence. Because of it, people think they can dispose of themselves as they wish. We are free, they say. Yes, we are free, but within limits. We are free to fulfill the divine will. Never can license be allowed, but only the freedom which makes us sons of God, that freedom which is truly worthy of Christians. Too often one is dominated by one's feelings!

Day by day this gift of counsel must enlighten us to select only what is pleasing to God.

St. Paul is a great example of docility to God's will. When he was thrown down from his horse and realized that the One appearing to him was Jesus Christ, he asked: "What is it I must do, sir?" (Acts 22:10) He asked the Lord, but what reply did he receive? Jesus did not tell him what to do. Instead He arranged for one of His disciples to tell him: "Get up and go into Damascus. There you will be told about everything you are destined to do" (Acts 22:10).

He who will have fulfilled the will of God will receive the reward, the recompense, but what reward will he receive who does his own will? God rewards what is done according to His will.

Of what use would it be to be baptized if afterwards we were to do our own will? Of what use would it be to recite the "Our Father"?

At times we might feel distaste or an urge to rebel inwardly when we are told the will of God; we might even shed tears. Nevertheless, if we turn to God, saying: "Not my will, but Yours be done," we will receive

His blessing. When God guides us along a path, He sows His graces there.

God's will is always accompanied by His help, by His blessings. Wherever we follow our own choice, our own will, we find thorns without consolations. When, instead, we proceed according to the will of God, we encounter some thorns (as Jesus was crowned with them), but we enjoy intimate consolations and our work succeeds.

Let us be wise! May the Holy Spirit enlighten us!

Some might say: "I have my own conscience!" But one might have an erroneous conscience.... The Gospel tells us that Jesus was subject to Mary and Joseph: "He was subject to them."

The gift of *fortitude* is a permanent virtue which the Holy Spirit communicates to our will in order to strengthen it and dispose it to do good in spite of every difficulty. Fortitude has two outstanding characteristics: endurance in great sufferings and ability to do great things.

He who resolves to attain sanctity and daily starts anew, notwithstanding temptations, exterior difficulties and perhaps even weaknesses and falls, saying: "Today I will begin again"—such a person possesses fortitude.

He who dedicates himself to his mission and moves steadily ahead, neither looking to the left nor to the right at the obstacles in his way, possesses fortitude.

Because we are weak and inclined to evil, let us draw near the Divine Master. In the Garden of Gethsemane He confessed His weakness: "The spirit is willing, but the flesh is weak" (Mt. 26:42-43). Isn't this our problem? How many resolutions we make.... But by admitting our weakness, we become strong through the grace of God. Let us look at our leader, Jesus Christ, and imitate Him. What great sufferings He underwent! Let us study the lives of Mary, the strong woman, and of all the saints. They suffered many afflictions and temptations and derived great profit from them.

It is well to recall the effect which the Holy Spirit produced in the apostles after His descent upon them in the Cenacle. What a change in Peter, who during the passion had been frightened by a woman's accusation! Now, after being filled with the Holy Spirit, he gave a talk, fearlessly facing all dangers, and clearly manifesting his ardent love for Jesus Christ.

It is very helpful to reflect upon St. Paul's fortitude, too. His entire life was a manifestation of fortitude, but we will only refer to the episode that occurred when Paul was on his way to Jerusalem. Upon arriving at Miletus he sent word to Ephesus, summoning the presbyters of that Church. And when they came to him, he delivered this address:

"Now, as you see, I am on my way to Jerusalem, compelled by the Spirit and not knowing what will happen to me there — except that the Holy Spirit has been warning me from city to city that chains and hardships await me. I put no value on my life if only I can finish my race and complete the service to which I have been assigned by the Lord Jesus, bearing witness to the Gospel of God's grace" (Acts 20:17-25).

Through the Holy Spirit Paul knew that great trials awaited him in Jerusalem. Did this stop him? Did he avoid going to Jerusalem? On the contrary, he imitated Jesus who, when the time of His passion was drawing near, walked faster toward Jerusalem, the site of His martyrdom.

Whose sons are we? When reflecting on the lives of those who had preceded them, early Christians would exclaim: "We are the sons of the martyrs!"

Do we have something to suffer? Let us offer it up for heaven. The thought of heaven is enough to give us courage! "So great is the good that awaits me, that every pain becomes a delight," St. Francis of Assisi would exclaim.

The gift of *wisdom* is a supernatural light of the Holy Spirit revealing how the truths of faith are worthy to be believed. It shows them to be acceptable even for reasons of the natural order, and it leads us to look heavenward — above the things of this earth.

When the psalmist says:

"O Lord, our Lord,
> how glorious is your name over all the earth" (Ps. 8:1)

he rises from the earth to the Creator. How admirable is Your name; that is, how great are Your works! The heavens magnify Your power. The order of creation, in fact, the very things of creation show us that You made everything, that everything comes from You. You disposed the numbers, weight and size of everything that exists and ordained everything to one end only: that creation might give You praise and, praising You, find its joy.

All creatures, even the inanimate, the mute, speak to one who has the gift of wisdom. The little blossom opening in the morning, the bird singing, the immense ocean, the high mountains, and all that has taken place and is taking place in history — everything speaks of the all-wise God. In creating us, He manifested who He is, for creation is a revelation. Blessed is he who reads the book of creation.

Let us adore God in the marvelous spectacles of nature. "The Lord has made everything for his own ends" (Prv. 16:4).

Let us lift up our heart to God in gratitude for the gift of life, the gift of being a Christian, of being preserved in life and given the grace of a religious vocation.

Divine Providence is with us at every moment, in both the order of nature and in the order of grace.

Let us ask our Lord's pardon for not having been sufficiently grateful for the benefits we have received.

We have so many gifts: the Eucharistic Sacrifice, the sacraments, the bread of the divine Word, our apostolate, the daily help of those who care for us. Let us be grateful to God, love Him and correspond to all these graces!

We can even reap good from the mistakes we make. If history is the teacher of humanity, our personal experience is a teacher to each of us.

We can always learn new lessons. It can be said that one year teaches the next, if we are attentive. And remembering our past mistakes, we should walk with greater humility, pray more, try to be more vigilant and avoid the company of those who might lead us to do wrong.

On the other hand, reflecting on the fact that God has had so much patience with us until now should lead us to love Him more and to resolve to serve Him more faithfully. Each morning, when we look at the calendar, we should repeat: "I must strive for heaven: may I spend today in a holy manner!" The daily performance of our duties is a continual hymn of love we offer to the Blessed Trinity.

Let us often ask the Holy Spirit for the gift of wisdom.

The gift of *piety* leads us to honor and love God as our Father and to place filial confidence in Him.

When one possesses the gift of piety, the liturgy of the Mass, Holy Communion, and the Visit to the Blessed Sacrament acquire a special meaning. The true spirit of piety leads to love of the Blessed Virgin as our Mother and to intimacy with Jesus. At times we read certain expressions of the saints which might seem a bit exaggerated, but those expressions came from the heart, the heart of a saint. It was the gift of piety which led them to speak that way.

When one possesses the gift of piety, even if external circumstances bring about a change in schedule, he performs his practices of piety despite sacrifice.

The gift of piety makes us fear to offend God because we love Him as a Father and therefore will not offend Him by sinning, not even venially. Rather, we are delicate of conscience and feel the need of making reparation. The gift of piety makes us feel sad if someone denies the divinity of Jesus, if scandal is given to the young, or if souls are in crisis. Jesus said: "My heart is moved with pity for the crowd" (Mk. 8:2). Zeal is spontaneous. One feels compassion for souls and desires to help them in every way possible. And when one no longer can work, there is still the apostolate of prayer, the apostolate of suffering, the apostolate of example. These are apostolates which are always possible in every circumstance and condition of life.

Let us therefore ask for the gift of piety in order to pray with the spirit of filial love of God and carry out our apostolate with brotherly love.

The gift of *fear of the Lord* drives away sin and leads one to respect the justice of God, His majesty and goodness.

Jesus rejected Satan, but man has not. Jesus answered him: "Begone, Satan!" The time has come for apostles inflamed with love of God to resist the devil and say: "Get behind me, Satan!"

Cast sin from the earth!

Jesus Christ, the Son of God, became incarnate to wipe out iniquity.

In order to banish sin from the world, new apostles must be inflamed with the fire of divine love — the same fire which filled the apostles and Mary while they prayed in the Cenacle. Let us humbly pray that Jesus may renew that divine Pentecost.

The fear of the Lord may also be considered in relation to the sins of one's past life and in relation to the future.

With regard to the past, the Holy Spirit infuses sorrow for sin — not just a natural sorrow, but a supernatural one.

Sorrow for sin is a gift of God. We should ask of the Holy Spirit perfect sorrow for sin. Devout souls do not find this hard. Think of St. Augustine in his *Confessions!* What self-accusation and, above all, what repentance and resolution! How his life changed! What good he worked in the Church, in souls, after his conversion!

Moreover, the fear of the Lord must keep sin away from us in the future.

We must cast sin from our lives with a firm will to sin no more and the resolve to take the necessary means to avoid it, that is, "vigilance and prayer."

Let us ask, therefore, for the gift of fear of the Lord. This is the last in the list, but it is the basis for obtaining the other gifts.

Consecration to the Holy Spirit

O divine Holy Spirit, eternal Love of the Father and of the Son, I adore You, I thank You, I love You, and I ask You pardon for all the times I have grieved You in myself and in my neighbor.

Descend with many graces during the holy ordination of bishops and priests, during the consecration of men and women religious, during the reception of confirmation by all the faithful; be light, sanctity and zeal.

To You, O Spirit of Truth, I consecrate my mind, imagination and memory; enlighten me. May I know Jesus Christ our Master and understand His Gospel and the teaching of Holy Church. Increase in me the gifts of wisdom, knowledge, understanding and counsel.

To You, O sanctifying Spirit, I consecrate my will. Guide me in Your will, sustain me in the observance of the commandments, in the fulfillment of my duties. Grant me the gifts of fortitude and holy fear of God.

To You, O life-giving Spirit, I consecrate my heart. Guard and increase the divine life in me. Grant me the gift of piety. Amen.

Contemplating
Jesus and Mary
in the Rosary

"By means of devout contemplation, the rosary recalls to the mind of the person praying the mysteries of the life of Christ, and stimulates the will to draw from them the norms of living.

"Mary, the New Woman, stands at the side of Christ, the New Man.

"Devotion to the Mother of the Lord is an opportunity for growing in divine grace, which is friendship with God, communion with Him, and the indwelling of the Holy Spirit."

—Pope Paul VI

THE JOYFUL MYSTERIES
First Joyful Mystery
The Annunciation of the Archangel to Mary

JESUS IN THE ROSARY—The Messiah

Messiah means the "one sent." After a long period of expectation on the part of mankind, Jesus came to live among men in order to redeem them from sin, save them from hell and reopen heaven to them. Let us give thanks to God.

MARY IN THE ROSARY — Mary's Privileges

Let us picture the most holy Virgin, humble and hidden, praying in the house of Nazareth, asking God to send the Savior. She was most humble, and thus merited to be chosen as Mother of God. Let us contemplate her and seek to imitate her fervor and great humility. Mary called herself the handmaid of the Lord, and He employed this faithful handmaid as a docile instrument of salvation.

Second Joyful Mystery
Mary's Visit to St. Elizabeth

JESUS IN THE ROSARY — Jesus, Our Life

Jesus is the life of our soul. He Himself said it: "I am the way, and the truth, and the life" (Jn. 14:6). He lives in the Holy Eucharist. He is the vine, we are the branches. Only by remaining united to Him will we have life: "Apart from me, you can do nothing" (Jn. 15:5).

"I myself am the living bread
come down from heaven....
He who feeds on my flesh
and drinks my blood
has life eternal" (Jn. 6:51, 54).

MARY IN THE ROSARY — Mediatrix of Graces

Where Mary enters, consolation enters. Mary is the channel through which all graces come to us. She is the stair and connecting link between Jesus and us. Upon her arrival, the hospitable house of her cousin was blessed; St. John was sanctified; Zechariah later regained his speech; and Elizabeth, filled with the Holy Spirit, prophesied.... Mary brings and distributes graces wherever she goes. Let us do everything with Mary, in Mary, and for Mary, often repeating the short act of consecration: "I am all Yours and all that I have I offer to You, my loving Jesus, through Mary, Your most holy Mother."

Third Joyful Mystery
The Birth of Jesus
in the Stable of Bethlehem

JESUS IN THE ROSARY – Jesus, Our Way

Jesus is our model. He, the Divine Master, begins His school in the stable of Bethlehem. From the stable He gives us lessons in poverty, humility and the spirit of sacrifice. Let us follow the way He has pointed out to us. It is the way that leads to heaven, where He reigns with His faithful followers.

MARY IN THE ROSARY – Mother of God

Mary's divine maternity is a truth of faith. Let us imagine ourselves in Bethlehem among the shepherds and the magi. See how Mary adores Jesus – her acts of faith, of love, of reparation.... She looks at Him, kisses

Him, presses Him to her heart. Let us prostrate ourselves before the crib to adore the Infant Jesus and obtain from the most holy Virgin permission to hold Him in our arms and confide all to Him. He is a wise Infant, who knows everything and everyone.

Fourth Joyful Mystery
The Presentation of Jesus in the Temple

JESUS IN THE ROSARY—Eternal Priest

The priest is the "dispenser of the mysteries of God." Pray for holy priests for the glory of God, the spread of the Faith, the sanctification of all the faithful.

MARY IN THE ROSARY—Model of Virtue

Mary was most conscientious in carrying out all exercises of devotion—so much so that, even though not obliged, she chose to act as all other women did by presenting Jesus in the Temple. Her humility and spirit of poverty shone forth in her offering of doves, the gift of the poor. Let us ask for Mary's love for true piety.

Fifth Joyful Mystery
The Losing and Finding of Jesus

JESUS IN THE ROSARY—The Master

Jesus chose His divine mission. In the eyes of men, He was a carpenter, but His mission was actually quite different. He opened His divine school in the Temple, where He explained the Sacred Scriptures and astonished everyone with His wisdom. He sat in the midst of the doctors as master, and they listened to Him. Jesus is the eternal Master by nature, by choice, by profession.

MARY IN THE ROSARY — The Heart of Mary Without Jesus

When she discovered that she had lost Jesus, Mary gave herself no peace. She sought Him everywhere, asked everyone.... What anxiety there was in her heart! How much she suffered until she found Him! When Jesus is hidden from us, we should seek Him as Mary did.

THE SORROWFUL MYSTERIES
First Sorrowful Mystery
Jesus Prays in the Garden of Gethsemane

JESUS IN THE ROSARY — The Savior's Patience

Jesus suffered until He sweat blood. He knew that His sufferings would give glory to the Eternal Father and good to men; therefore, He willingly accepted the bitter chalice: "Not my will, but yours be done" (Lk. 22:42). Let us try to console Jesus by avoiding sin, so as not to renew His sufferings.

MARY IN THE ROSARY — The Sorrowful Mother

The life of the Blessed Mother was a long martyrdom. Let us often meditate on the sorrows of the Queen of Martyrs, our Sorrowful Mother. It is a practice that is very pleasing to her — one that she will reward with precious and abundant graces.

Second Sorrowful Mystery
The Scourging of Jesus

JESUS IN THE ROSARY — Jesus Makes Reparation for Us

To make reparation for the sins of men, Jesus received the punishment in His own holy body. By mortifying His flesh, He obtained for us the grace to place our flesh, our passions, under the dominion of our spirit.

MARY IN THE ROSARY — The Most Pure Virgin

Mary was virgin in body and in spirit. In her the spirit always dominated, never the flesh. She merited to enter into heaven soul *and* body, because she was the Virgin most pure.

Third Sorrowful Mystery
The Crowning with Thorns

JESUS IN THE ROSARY — Christ the King

Let us make reparation for the insults Jesus received from the soldiers who mocked

His kingship. May we let Him reign in our hearts with His love! Let us pray that Jesus Christ will reign in every individual, in every family, throughout society.

MARY IN THE ROSARY — The Graces of Mary
The Blessed Mother wants her children to be holy, and she prefers to give them spiritual graces. Whoever confides in her and asks her help finds that she always responds with new graces.

Fourth Sorrowful Mystery
Jesus Is Condemned to Death

JESUS IN THE ROSARY — King of Martyrs
Jesus was the first to walk the way of sorrows, and how many heroes, how many martyrs, have followed Him! Pilate condemned Jesus. He saw and believed that Jesus was innocent and just, yet, because of human respect he condemned Him. Let us not imitate the baseness of Pilate who offended God so as not to displease men.

MARY IN THE ROSARY — Co-Redemptrix
Having learned that Jesus had been condemned to death, Mary went to meet Him. What anguish could be seen in their reciprocal gaze! The Blessed Virgin, Co-redemptrix of the human race, suffered in

heart and spirit the same torments that Jesus suffered in His body. Let us increase our hope that she who suffered so much for love of us will give us all the graces and help we need.

Fifth Sorrowful Mystery
The Crucifixion and Death of Jesus

JESUS IN THE ROSARY — Victim for Us
One who sacrifices himself, humbles himself, and gives his life for the good of others is a victim. "Now it is finished" (Jn. 19:30), Jesus said. Let us contemplate the painful scene of Calvary in the company of St. John, the Blessed Mother and the holy women, making their sentiments ours.

MARY IN THE ROSARY — Our Mother
In His testament of love, the dying Jesus left His holy Mother to be our Mother. Let us thank Jesus for this great favor and make the most of it. May we greatly love this Mother, imitate her, and be true children of hers, so that she may truly be our Mother.

THE GLORIOUS MYSTERIES
First Glorious Mystery
The Resurrection of Our Lord Jesus Christ

JESUS IN THE ROSARY—His Divinity

The miracle of the resurrection is the greatest proof of the divinity of Jesus Christ. Do we wish to share in His glory?

Let us die to ourselves, to our self-will, and we, too, will resurrect gloriously one day.

MARY IN THE ROSARY—The Joys of Mary

"Queen of Heaven, rejoice!" Mary's great sorrow over the passion of Jesus is succeeded by the great joy of His resurrection. Let us be strong during the sorrows of this painful exile so we will share in the joys of the final triumph.

Second Glorious Mystery
The Ascension of Jesus

JESUS IN THE ROSARY—Head of the Elect

Jesus Himself said: "I am indeed going to prepare a place for you" (Jn. 14:3). Whoever follows Jesus in life, will go to be with Him in heaven and enjoy Him for all eternity.

MARY IN THE ROSARY—The Spiritual Ascensions of Mary

After Jesus had ascended into heaven, Mary's soul had no other desire or wish than that of following her Jesus, of being with Him in heaven. How many acts of love and what fervent Communions Mary made during this time! Let us learn from the Blessed Virgin how to lift ourselves up by thinking of heaven.

Third Glorious Mystery
The Descent of the Holy Spirit

JESUS IN THE ROSARY—His Spirit

The Spirit of the Divine Master is the Spirit of love towards the Father—a fire that purifies, inflames hearts with fervor, sanctifies souls. Let us ask for an outpouring of the Holy Spirit.

MARY IN THE ROSARY—Queen of Apostles

It was through Mary and through her prayers that the apostles received the Holy Spirit. Let us, too, ask through her intercession the gifts and precious fruits of the Holy Spirit.

Fourth Glorious Mystery
The Assumption of Mary Most Holy

JESUS IN THE ROSARY—Comforter of the Dying

When death strikes, Jesus—faithful Brother and Friend—does not abandon one who loves Him. Rather, He goes to this person as Viaticum, to give him strength and courage, to console him during his last hours. Jesus was sweet comfort for His holy Mother, who left this earth in an intense and strong impetus of love. Jesus will comfort the dying in proportion to the intensity with which they have loved Him during life.

MARY IN THE ROSARY — External Devotion to Mary
   Let us renew our devotion to the most holy Virgin and venerate her by frequent participation in public and private acts of devotion held in her honor.

Fifth Glorious Mystery
The Coronation of Mary Most Holy

JESUS IN THE ROSARY — Jesus, Our Reward
   Jesus will be our eternal reward, as He was the reward of our Blessed Mother: "I shall be your great reward in heaven."

MARY IN THE ROSARY — Devotion to the Blessed Mother
   True devotion to the Blessed Mother should be practiced as St. Louis de Montfort taught it: that is, by doing all in Mary, with Mary and through Mary, approaching Jesus with her help. He who loves Mary in this way will certainly become a saint.

The
Joyful
Mysteries
and
Religious Life

Loving God Above All Things

In the joyful mysteries we may ask for the grace to observe the vow of poverty; in the sorrowful, the vow of chastity; in the glorious, the vow of obedience.

These reflections will first consider the vow of poverty. The vow's meaning is known from the constitutions of the Institute. Poverty is, as it were, a point of departure for progress in religious perfection. Our Lord chose to begin His earthly life in poverty and to utter His first beatitude for the poor.

Let us ask ourselves: What is poverty? Is it only detachment from earthly goods?

It is both detachment from the things of this world and a striving for those of heaven. Instead of earthly goods, we must seek the highest Good: God. Through poverty we use the goods and things of this world as means for acquiring those which are eternal. At the point of death, we will leave everything behind, and only if we have sought God will we attain Him. Therefore, a person loves poverty in the full sense if he or she is attached to God, seeks God and uses the things of this earth insofar as they are useful to attaining God.

"Woe to you rich," exclaimed Jesus, "for your consolation is now" (Lk. 6:24). "Blest are you poor; the reign of God is yours" (Lk. 6:20).

Those unfortunates who pursue worldly pleasures content themselves with what is fleeting, with what they can enjoy day by day. Yet they know that at the end they will lose all. The religious, on the other hand, seeks what will never perish—the kingdom of God and his personal sanctification: "Seek first his kingship over you, his way of holiness, and all these things will be given you besides..." (Mt. 6:33).

There was a certain man who found a great treasure hidden in a field. He returned home and quietly sold everything he had in order to accumulate enough money to buy the field. By purchasing the field, he acquired the treasure.

It is wisdom—great wisdom—to leave passing goods to gain the eternal, to leave temporary enjoyment to gain merit for eternity. When a person makes the vow of poverty with wisdom, appreciating its value, he is liberated from the preoccupations of dress, lodging, nourishment, etc.—the preoccupations of this world. He lifts himself towards God, like an eagle soaring towards the heights.

In the first joyful mystery, we contemplate the annunciation of the archangel Gabriel to Mary. The angel was sent by the heavenly Father to a poor village that no one esteemed: "Can anything good come from Nazareth?" (Jn. 1:46) He was sent into a poor little house to a poor virgin — Mary. Notice God's preferences! When the Son of God was to become incarnate, He sought the virgin who was the most holy, the most rich in merit, the Immaculate, she who abounded in virtue and in grace. The Lord did not send the archangel to the palace of the Caesars, nor even to the wealthy homes of Jerusalem or any luxurious dwelling, but rather to a poor, little house, stripped of everything, inhabited by a most holy virgin.

Mary understood the spirit of God and the divine preferences! Notice whom she appeared to at Lourdes — not to a wealthy girl, but to Bernadette, who was ignorant, sickly and from a very poor family, and who was searching for wood because of the cold and the poverty of their house.

When the Blessed Virgin appeared at Fatima, it was to three poor, little shepherds who were pasturing their flock. One who desires graces knows what Jesus' and Mary's preferences are — the spirit of poverty. Mary seeks the poor in spirit to give them her graces; God seeks the poor in spirit to give His graces and communicate His heavenly treasures.

The second joyful mystery presents for our consideration Mary's swift journey to Elizabeth's house. She traversed many miles on foot, through mountainous country, not because she wanted to be recognized as Mother of God, but because she knew that Elizabeth needed her help at that time. Mary remained there for three months, as long as Elizabeth needed her, and the services she rendered in that house were performed humbly, in the conditions of a poor person who serves. How often we adopt certain attitudes and gestures which surely do not show that we have the spirit of poverty and detachment that one ought to have in religious life.

We want to become like Jesus and Mary; hence, let us reflect on the third mystery — the birth of Jesus. Where was Jesus born? In a cave; not in a city but in a stable, that is, a place meant for animals. The Son of God born in a stable! And He was placed in a manger, on the straw. Whom did the angels call to adore Him? They called the shepherds — poor, simple, coarse men — and it was they who gave the first offerings. And Jesus began to live on charity.

We let ourselves be overcome by the temptation to have fine things, and there is also a little too much care given to food, too much concern about having conveniences, and attachment to the place where one is. A book I read a few days ago said to attach oneself neither to a place nor to an activity. There was an example of a priest returning from the missions, already old and worn out. His superior asked him, "If you had to set out again for India, how much time would you need to get ready?"

"Three hours," the missionary replied. But he corrected himself at once. "No, no. Not even a minute. I would go right away and gladly."

We must become detached from occupations, places and even life itself; this, then, is the highest degree of poverty — to die when God wishes it and in the circumstances He wishes. I was greatly edified on one occasion when I had to take a plane in very bad weather and it seemed that the trip would be quite hazardous. The Sister with whom I was traveling said, "Even if we had to die this way, what would it matter, if it is God's will?"

One does God's will when one goes to perform a duty promptly and lovingly.

In the fourth mystery Jesus is brought to the Temple to be offered to God, as was the Hebrew custom. What price of redemption did Mary and Joseph bring? The Gospel notes that the poor would offer a pair of turtledoves or two young pigeons. And this was the offering of Mary and Joseph for the redemption of Jesus—the offering of the poor, whereas the rich had to offer more. Sometimes, instead of being content to possess nothing, one feels ashamed of being poor. Mary and Joseph were not ashamed to show themselves poor, either to the priests or to the people around them.

In the fifth mystery we recall that without the knowledge of Mary and Joseph the twelve-year-old Jesus remained in the Temple to talk with the learned men. His questions and answers showed His wisdom and the mission that He was one day to carry out in homage to His heavenly Father. He manifested His great wisdom and was admired. The Gospel notes that right after this episode, Jesus returned to His ordinary life of obedience. In the company of Mary and Joseph, He returned to Nazareth and "was obedient to them" until the age of thirty in the humble life of a carpenter. The Gospel places these two facts side by side—the wisdom Jesus displayed and His humility and poverty of spirit in doing the work of a carpenter for eighteen years. He was the local carpenter, and whoever needed His work came to Him. Let us imagine Him from the age of twelve to the age of thirty, bent over the bench of that difficult trade, with those calloused hands that worked for Himself and for His family. Pope Leo XIII wrote: "The angels of heaven drew near that poor house to see the Son of God, the Lord of all, working to earn His bread."

Work is detachment from the things of the earth and the point of departure for sanctification. Without it, the soul will always turn towards what is lower; it will make some efforts and in some moments of fervor will try to elevate itself, but then it will fall back, striving in vain to rise, like the bird that is tied. Why doesn't it fall in love with God, attach itself to Him?

Attachments to little things are like the meshes of a net that block progress. Hence, the need of carefully examining whether we have this spirit of religious poverty.

The perfection of poverty goes to the point of detachment from life. This is reached gradually by detaching oneself from positions, places, friends and occupations and trying to attain perfect indifference, to attain this one, sole desire: "My God and my all." The ejaculation that Pope Pius XI never ceased repeating — "God alone is enough for me" — should be the foundation of our life. Whatever we have on earth is all for use. When we die, others will take it; others will live in the house and room where we lived; others will carry out our duty. Therefore, let us not lose merits through attachments!

Some persons seem to reason well, but when they come to such considerations as these, they lose not only the spirit of faith but also their accuracy of reasoning. Let us ask Jesus and Mary for the spirit of poverty; let us learn perfect detachment through the examples of their lives. A saint says that the happiness of a religious consists in not having anything and that his unhappiness consists in having something that may constitute the center of his affections and imperceptibly make him lose the joy and peace of abandonment in God.

Why, when they begin to have possessions, do religious lose the great virtue of trust? That great attribute of God — His Providence — must always be honored! Let us trust in Him and recall what Christ said in this regard: "Look at the birds in the sky. They do not sow or reap, they gather nothing into barns; yet your heavenly Father feeds them.... Learn a lesson from the way the wild flowers grow. They do not work; they do not spin. Yet I assure you, not even Solomon in all his splendor was arrayed like one of these.... Is not the body more valuable than clothes?" (Mt. 6:25-29)

Often vanity halts the journey towards perfection. Reasonable care should be had for the body, insofar as it serves the soul and the soul perfects itself in communion with the body.

When will we love God above all things? When saying the joyful mysteries, then, let us have the intention of wanting to progress in the virtue of poverty.

The
Sorrowful
Mysteries
and
Religious Life

"I Have Chosen You"

On God's part, a vocation to the religious life is a choice made out of love for certain of His creatures. On our part, it is an act of perfect, continuous, everlasting love. It is love that goes directly to God, without any intermediary.

In the sorrowful mysteries of the rosary, let us ask the observance of the vow of chastity and the perfection of the corresponding virtue.

On the whole, the sorrowful mysteries are those which portray the reparation Jesus made for sin, especially for sins against chastity. Moreover, through His sorrowful mysteries the Lord obtained for us the grace to observe the vow and practice the virtue of chastity. We also know that the most holy Virgin shared in the passion as Co-redemptrix and through this participation acquired a right to a power before God to obtain the virtue of chastity for those devoted to her.

Failings against chastity may take place in the heart, in the mind, in the will, in the internal and external senses.

Jesus made satisfaction for all the failings that could be committed in these ways, and He has given us the grace to be able to keep ourselves pure in mind, will and heart.

The virtue of chastity makes a person dear to God. Something extraordinary, not observed in the worldly, emanates from one who is chaste. Moreover, chastity is essential to the religious life, and the latter cannot be spoken of without it. When kept, the Constitutions of the Institute protect chastity from harm, since they provide the means necessary to guard it.

In the Our Father we say: "Lead us not into temptation," but often it is we who lead ourselves into temptation. "Everyone knows," observes Pope Paul VI, "that in the present condition of human society the practice of perfect chastity is made difficult, not only because of the prevalence of depraved morality but also on account of false teachings which glamorize excessively the merely natural condition of man." Some individuals place themselves in the occasions of evil and have no right to God's help, to His grace; instead, others, permitted by God to undergo trials and temptations, are accompanied by His grace.

In the first sorrowful mystery we contemplate Jesus in agony in the garden of Gethsemane. Three kinds of suffering weighed upon His heart: first, His approaching passion, the humiliations and pain that He would have to endure, the death He was to undergo, the desertion of His disciples and the momentary triumph of His enemies; second, all the sins of mankind, which He was taking upon Himself, becoming "like unto sin"; third, those who would still be lost, notwithstanding His sufferings: "What gain would there be from my lifeblood?" (Ps. 30:10)

Weighed down with these thoughts and emotions, Jesus felt almost overwhelmed by sorrow. His heart endured all the anguish of that moment; He sweat blood because of the torment of His spirit and heart, yet He declared nonetheless: "Father...not my will but yours be done" (Lk. 22:42). In this way He atoned for all evil sentiments, all sins committed with the heart—even desires, aversions, attractions and every inordinate inclination.

In the second sorrowful mystery Jesus is tied to a pillar and struck by His tormentors with tremendous blows from the scourges until He is reduced to the state described by the prophet:

"From the sole of the foot to the head
 there is no sound spot:
Wound and welt and gaping gash,
 not drained, or bandaged,
 or eased with salve" (Is. 1:6).

How affectionately we must kiss the most sacred heart of Jesus as we reflect that in that way He especially atoned for sins of touch—the most widespread of the body's senses, the one with which external sins against purity are most easily committed. Let us kneel before Jesus, reduced as He is to one, great wound, and ask of Him the strength to resist and combat evil, to mortify our senses with work, effort and bodily discipline, whether in public or in private.

The third sorrowful mystery reminds us of Jesus' atonement for the sins of impure thoughts. The crown of thorns that had been placed on His head was struck by sticks and reeds so that the thorns would penetrate more deeply.

Unfortunately, some thoughts, fancies, daydreams and memories are not too pure! Let us reflect, in the first place, upon the interior, because sin always begins in the mind. In this regard, Pope Paul VI says, "It is evident that the proper way of living religious life requires discipline. Therefore, the life of the religious should find no place for books, periodicals or shows which are unbecoming or indecent, not even under the pretext of a desire to learn things useful to know or to broaden one's education, except possibly the case, duly ascertained by the religious superior, where there is proven necessity for the study of such things. In a world pervaded by so many sordid forms of vice, no one can adequately reckon the powerful effectiveness of the sacred ministry of one whose life is radiant with the light of a chastity consecrated to God and from which he draws his strength."

In the fourth sorrowful mystery Jesus is condemned to death—condemned by a man having authority, it is true, yet by a sinner like all others. We must reflect: Jesus took the cross on His shoulders and carried it to Calvary: "If a man wishes to come after me, he must deny his very self, take up his cross, and begin to follow in my footsteps" (Mt. 16:24). This means mortification. "Put to death whatever in your nature is rooted in earth," says St. Paul (Col. 3:5).

The fifth sorrowful mystery recalls for us the crucifixion of Jesus. On Calvary Jesus was stripped of His garments. The tunic was gambled away and the other garments were divided among the executioners, in reparation for vanity and inordinate self-satisfaction. Jesus was also given gall and myrrh to drink. The palate must be mortified; one must be temperate, whether by sometimes taking what is not pleasing or by mortifying oneself a little in what one likes most.

Jesus was made to stretch Himself out upon the cross and extend His hands in conformity to its shape. And are hands always in place? His feet were nailed to the cross. And do we walk where we could find danger? Have all our steps always been holy?

On the cross Jesus asked His Father's pardon for His crucifiers and died amid the people's insults and in bodily agony. Because of Jesus' death on the cross, we ask this grace: to preserve purity intact, since a person who goes to hell goes either because of the sin of impurity or at least not without it. Let us address our prayers to the wounded Jesus, so that through the sufferings of His passion He will give us the grace to avoid all evil occasions and always to live with our body in check: "for fear that after having preached to others I myself should be rejected" (1 Cor. 9:27).

Let us often kiss the crucifix, for in kissing it we arouse ourselves to love, and when one is in love with Jesus he feels the flesh and temptation less and will be spiritually fruitful in the world.

The
Glorious
Mysteries
and
Religious Life

Growing in Grace and Wisdom

Continuing our reflections on the mysteries of the rosary, with the glorious mysteries we will consider the life of Christ under the aspect of obedience, in order to grow with Him in wisdom and grace.

Obedience is of the mind, conforming one's judgment; of the heart, conforming one's sentiments promptly; and of execution. It must be said that often the obedience of religious is a semi-obedience of the mind, heart, execution, energy, activity. One doesn't want to disobey, but meanwhile he does as he wants, at least in part.

The bases of obedience are three: the natural law for a society, the domestic authority of the superiors, and also the power that is called dominative. These powers are recognized when one makes the vow of obedience. May obedience not begin to diminish little by little with the passing of the years!

How can we ask the virtue of obedience in the glorious mysteries?

In this way: Jesus and Mary obeyed, and because of this they were exalted.

Jesus was obedient in His private life: "He was obedient to them" (Lk. 2:51); and in His public life: "I always do what pleases him" (Jn. 8:29).

Obedience is a humiliation. We must submit our judgment, our will, and our whole being with joy, even if all this is repugnant. Certain religious want their superiors to discuss with them regarding what is pleasing or less pleasing, in such a way that both superior and subject give in a little in the course of the discussion. They say that this conformism of obedience, as they have defined it, is suited to the democratic times in which we live.

Pope Pius XII spoke out very strongly against this theory, which annuls the religious life, inasmuch as obedience is the keystone without which religious life cannot stand. If the beams for supporting the roof are missing, a building will crumble; the same thing will happen to an institute if obedience is missing.

Obedience is a humiliation—perhaps the greatest humiliation required in the religious life. To encourage ourselves, we must always look to Jesus, the God-man, who obeyed Joseph and Mary and even His crucifiers. "He emptied himself and took the form of a slave, being born in the likeness of men" (Phil. 2:7). This is the point to which Jesus' obedience extended! When obedience costs us a little, we line up reasons for dispensing ourselves or perhaps judge and condemn and also give bad example by criticizing and objecting, without noticing that the walls of the building are breaking up, that the foundation is being ruined.

Jesus humiliated Himself even before His crucifiers, and the Father exalted Him. His enemies believed that they had triumphed over Him, but if at first He was reduced to one wound, see how each of His wounds transformed itself in the splendor of glory! Immortal and impassible, on the day of the ascension He lifted Himself towards heaven in the presence of the disciples and Mary and ascended into glory: "He sits at the right hand of the Father, in the glory of God the Father." The great reward of obedience is glorification, for the more we humiliate ourselves the more will we be exalted. And if one loves himself and desires to be glorious one day, let him humiliate himself greatly. This is our life. We must humiliate ourselves greatly in life and make the most of the opportunities that are not lacking during the day. Let us be conscientious, attentive to seize these opportunities. "Whoever humbles himself shall be exalted" (Mt. 23:12) — Jesus humiliated Himself as much as He could, and surely He could not call Himself a sinner!

Thus, let us humiliate ourselves if we want to have a high degree of glory in heaven.

Mary declared herself the servant of God and acted as such. She accompanied her Son to Calvary, undergoing the humiliation and mortification of being pointed out as the mother of a criminal. Who knows what comments the cruel throng made! Because of her humiliation, Mary was assumed into heaven; because of the humility of her entire life, she was crowned queen of the universe — that is, of heaven and earth.

The first glorification on earth comes about through holiness. The more a person advances in humility, the greater that person becomes in the eyes of God.

Mary
Mother of
Beautiful
Vocations

Mary Prepares the Ground
for Beautiful Vocations

Mary was greatly pleased to be called "Mother" by the Son of God; but the homage and prayers most pleasing to her after those of Jesus were those of the apostles. One who wants more apostles to carry out a fruitful apostolate and fails to ask them of Mary, works in vain.

One who wants to be an apostle and does not make Mary a part of his or her life, deprives himself or herself of an indispensable aid.

Let us consider the necessity of Mary in the life of the apostle and in the apostolate.

The apostle must be holy in order to sanctify; wise in order to instruct; and zealous in order to overcome the obstacles encountered.

The first field that the apostle must cultivate is his or her own soul. His first work is that of the interior life. The first soul to save is his own. The apostle must sanctify his mind in a faith which is ever more wise and living. He must sanctify his will in a docility ever more conformed to God's will. He must sanctify his heart in unity of desires, dispositions and life with the heart of Jesus. And he must sanctify his body, so that every one of its energies is reserved for God.

For all this, the apostle needs Mary. If devotion to Mary is morally necessary for salvation, it is all the more necessary for sanctification. If devotion to Mary is necessary for the faithful to live as good Christians and to observe the commandments, it is much more necessary in order to be apostles and observe the evangelical counsels.

If devotion to Mary is morally necessary for youth to overcome passion and reach heaven, so much the more necessary is it in order to aspire to perfect and perpetual chastity and lead other souls to heaven.

Therefore, Mary is the Mother of beautiful vocations. God has a style of action proper to Himself. He gave us Jesus Christ, Mediator and Apostle, through Mary.

When Mary pronounced her "Fiat," she became the mother of the great Priest, the mother of every beautiful vocation. She welcomed, nourished and clothed the best "vocation." She accompanied Him throughout His infancy, His private life, His public life. She assisted Him when He was dying and gave Him back to heaven in the Ascension.

Mary acts similarly with every soul called to the priesthood, to the religious life, to the apostolate.

Let all vocational work, therefore, be carried out by Mary, with Mary, in Mary and for Mary. Let the entire apostolate be carried out by Mary, through Mary, with Mary, and in Mary. Let every hope to promote the glory of God, the sanctification of the apostle and the salvation of souls be placed in Mary, by Mary, through Mary.

Of Mary, Queen of the Apostles, we ask laborers for the evangelical vineyard. Those who are called are to be entrusted to Mary during their youth and during their period of formation. Let our apostolic work be carried out with and in Mary.

We intend to close our eyes to the earthly light and open them to the perpetual light of heaven aided by Mary.

With Mary everything is easier, happier, holier and more fruitful. To Mary let us consecrate our entire selves, all the means of our apostolate and all our houses of formation.

It is the highest honor and the greatest merit for a family to be able to give a religious or priestly vocation to the Church, and this will be a great consolation at the point of death.

When you visit families, you too should infuse this hope. Life passes quickly. Parents have given physical life to their children, and the children in turn will obtain eternal life for their parents. The vocation is a grace, but through whose hands do graces pass? Through the hands of Mary.

The Assumption of Mary most holy has already been defined as a dogma of faith. Now efforts are being directed toward the definition of another dogma: that of Mary's universal mediation—in other words, the doctrine of Mary as Mediatrix of all graces. Before defining a dogma, the Church desires to reawaken the faithful to its spiritual meaning, which in this instance is the great good that Mary brings about in our lives.

Therefore, if Mary is the universal Mother of grace, she is especially the Mother of vocations. The vocation is the greatest and most beautiful grace; hence, why should it not pass through the hands of Mary? Priests and religious contribute to the salvation of the world, to the extension of the Church, the kingdom of God. And, in turn, priests or sisters are instrumental causes of other vocations. Through prayer, deeds, and writings, they arouse vocations and help those whom God calls to His service.

The most holy Virgin is the hope and trust of mankind. In prayer let us ask her to give parents the desire to have a vocation among their children. May she give them this ambition, this most noble aspiration...and also may she give them the grace to keep these flowers destined for the altar safe from sin.

May parents have a sense of their responsibility. If through malice they ruin their children's vocation, or if they refuse to give their children to God, will they, then, have the grace to save themselves? Say this to everyone and write it.

The first direct words of the boy Jesus that the Gospel records were those He pronounced in the Temple at the age of twelve, in order to defend His vocation and the rights of God: "Did you not know that I had to be in my Father's house?" (Lk. 2:49) And later, as soon as Jesus entered into His public ministry, He showed His interest in vocations and called the apostles to follow Him.

Ask of Mary the grace that vocations be formed well, that they may progress in piety, in love of God, in their desire to sanctify themselves. Pray for those who dedicate themselves to the recruiting or forming of vocations. "How useful it is to recite a 'Hail, Holy Queen' every morning to obtain the grace to recognize and direct beautiful vocations!" So said a fervent priest who had had much experience in a parish that had given many vocations to the Church.

Find vocations for the priesthood and religious life in grammar schools, high schools, colleges and universities, among youths in parish organizations, in truly Christian families. At all hours, let us leave workers behind us, thinking of the still uncultivated portions of the evangelical field.

To give vocations to the Church means to love the Church truly! To inspire vocations means to guarantee for ourselves the grace to correspond to our own. Let us feel with Christ the daily anxiety: "The harvest is great, but the laborers are few." Spreading devotion to Mary, Mother of God and Queen of the Apostles and of every apostolate, prepares the ground for beautiful vocations.

Also available from St. Paul Editions

A Call to Total Consecration
Very Rev. James Alberione, SSP, STD
Beginners and experienced religious alike will certainly treasure this inspiring and encouraging book which gives a deep understanding of the great privilege that is theirs.
94 pages; cloth $2.50; paper $1.50

Christ, Model and Reward of Religious
Very Rev. James Alberione, SSP, STD
"This book is deep, theological, stressing fundamentals in a beautiful way. The practical applications that are given are encouraging for those dedicated to a modern apostolate, clearly indicating the harmony between the essentials of a deep interior life and a dynamic apostolate in which the religious must never lose sight of her dedication." "Sponsa Regis"
208 pages; cloth $3.25

For Me To Live Is the Church
Rev. Elio Gambari, SMM
The ecclesiology of religious life. The raison d'etre of religious in the Church; the ecclesial vocation of the religious in its theological, priestly, prophetic, apostolic and juridical dimensions; the ecclesial religious personality; Mary, the prototype of religious life.
368 pages; cloth $5.00; paper $4.00

The Global Mystery of Religious Life
Rev. Elio Gambari, SMM
Delving deeply into the total picture of contemporary consecrated life, Father Gambari brings the full richness of Vatican II and post-conciliar documents to bear on this "gift of God." Especially directed to religious men and women, this first volume of the two-volume work, "Consecration and Service" (Vol. II, "Unfolding the Mystery of Religious Life"), clarifies the meaning of sound, on-going renewal, along with a vivid sketch of the valid forms which man's thrust toward union with God can take.
302 pages; cloth $5.00; paper $4.00

Glories and Virtues of Mary
Very Rev. James Alberione, SSP, STD
A moving presentation of Mary's heroic virtues and great privileges, drawn from Sacred Scripture and the Fathers of the Church.
251 pages; cloth $3.00; paper $2.00

Growing in Perfect Union
Very Rev. James Alberione, SSP, STD
"Father Alberione, as founder of several religious congregations, is exceptionally equipped for the task he sets before him: to provide religious not only with solid doctrine, upon which their vocations must be founded, but also to delineate for them practical guidelines for fruitful practice." "Spiritual Book News"
132 pages; cloth $3.00; paper $2.00

Lest We Forget
Very Rev. James Alberione, SSP, STD
Reflecting on the deceased brings: relief for those beloved souls, since we arouse ourselves to offer prayers and sacrifices for them; benefit for ourselves, because the thought of eternity helps us to shun sin and grow in perfection.
252 pages; cloth $3.00; paper $2.00

Journey Toward Renewal
Rev. Elio Gambari, SMM
Genuine renewal in religious life is interior dynamism, personality development, fidelity to one's own vocation, elimination of habitual mediocrity, attachment to one's own institute, maturation of baptismal grace, and progress in the priestly, prophetic, apostolic and ecclesial aspects of Christian life. Writing with firsthand knowledge and deep awareness of the needs and obligations of religious in the modern world, Father Gambari shows how renewal—growth in-depth in one's own vocation —involves an encounter with God, a prayerful clinging to His will, and an active response to the promptings of the Spirit.
200 pages; cloth $4.00; paper $3.00

Living Our Commitment
Very Rev. James Alberione, SSP, STD
In accord with the conciliar spirit of the decree "Adaptation and Renewal of Religious Life," Father Alberione has given a series of practical meditations on the cardinal and moral virtues so that the religious may attain to a more total living of his special commitment and a truly Christ-like personality.
168 pages, cloth $3.50; paper $2.50

Mary, Hope of the World
Very Rev. James Alberione, SSP, STD
A brilliant consideration of Mary under these aspects: in the mind of God, prophecies, and the longing of humanity; in her earthly life as Co-redemptrix of mankind; in her life of glory in heaven, in the Church and in the hearts of the faithful.
222 pages; cloth $3.00

Mary, Mother and Model
Very Rev. James Alberione, SSP, STD
The history and aim of 30 Marian feasts, their part in the Breviary, and the benefits to be derived from their observance. Illustrated.
237 pages; cloth $3.00; paper $2.00

Mary, Queen of Apostles
Very Rev. James Alberione, SSP, STD
On Mary's mission of giving Jesus to the world. Superb approach to the imitation of Mary in the apostolates of desires, prayer, example, suffering and action.
348 pages; cloth $4.00; paper $3.00

Meditation Notes on Paul the Apostle, Model of the Spiritual Life
Very Rev. James Alberione, SSP, STD
These writings of Father James Alberione, Founder of the Pauline Family, were discovered after his death in November, 1971. They are meditation notes and resolutions made during a course of spiritual exercises. The theme is St. Paul and the priest. Every priest and spiritual guide can find in these pages a great wealth of material.
100 pages; cloth $2.00

Month with St. Paul
Very Rev. James Alberione, SSP, STD
Rev. Timothy Giaccardo, SSP
This book of 31 inspiring meditations will bear frequent rereading and be of great spiritual help for priests, religious and for the laity. It is a true guide and consoler for those who are seeking spiritual happiness and perfection.
232 pages; paper $1.25

The Paschal Mystery and Christian Living
Very Rev. James Alberione, SSP, STD
Meditations on the passion, resurrection and ascension of the Lord Jesus designed to deepen the Christian's understanding of that pivotal event in time—the Paschal Mystery—and the event's transcendence of time and space to permeate the lives of each of us at every moment. An excellent volume of meditations for everyone—religious and laity alike—for to the living of this Mystery all of us are called.
200 pages; cloth $3.95; paper $2.95

Personality and Configuration with Christ
Very Rev. James Alberione, SSP, STD
Father Alberione's masterful and challenging blend of psychological insight and ageless wisdom. Writing in the spirit of the Second Vatican Council and emphasizing, as did Vatican II, the importance of the person, he presents step by step the process of personality development and fulfillment that culminates in the final goal of configuration with Christ, Way, Truth and Life.
192 pages; cloth $3.50; paper $2.50

Pray Always
Very Rev. James Alberione, SSP, STD
A solid and fundamental explanation of the need and value of prayer, various methods of speaking with God and the reward of closer living with God in daily life.
264 pages; cloth $3.00; paper $2.00

The Religious Adult in Christ
—Religious Formation before
    Perpetual Profession
Rev. Elio Gambari, SMM
This in-depth volume by an authority on religious life is devoted to the Juniorate and has two objectives: 1) to consider the Juniorate and its purpose; 2) to show that, no matter what it is called or when it is held, the Juniorate responds to an intrinsic formational need that is to be met at any cost.
306 pages; cloth $5.00; paper $4.00

Renewal in Religious Life
Rev. Elio Gambari, SMM
An authoritative guide with the answers to every problem of adaptation and renewal in religious life. Superiors, chapters, study groups, commissions and all those involved in any way in aggiornamento are calling for a handbook like this. Father Gambari takes up exactly what renewal entails for the individual religious and the entire institute; what can and cannot be changed; how to undertake the re-editing of the constitutions; how to update formation procedures. A source of fruitful reflection long after the flurry of aggiornamento has subsided.
400 pages; cloth $5.00; paper $4.00

The Superior Follows the Master
Very Rev. James Alberione, SSP, STD
The author shows a clear, deep understanding of religious community relations and his counsel is given with warm sympathy to superiors of religious women.
214 pages; paper $2.00

Thoughts
Very Rev. James Alberione, SSP, STD

The reader is introduced to the guidelines behind Father Alberione's amazing activity, evangelical spirit of prayer, and his far-seeing vision. This work of Father Alberione covers a wide range of topics: a vision of man and of history, Jesus Christ: center of thought and action, the presence of the Mother of God, St. Paul today, the Word of God, the Church, the Pope, vocations, prayer, the apostolate as a radiation of Christ, the media as a means of evangelization—all in his very original style, striking for its brevity and power.
211 pages; cloth $3.00

Unfolding the Mystery of Religious Life
Rev. Elio Gambari, SMM

The total on-going commitment of religious life to God and to the Church is a deep field for meditation. Following up the theme of volume one, "The Global Mystery of Religious Life," Father Gambari, in this second volume, examines in closer detail, the specific realities which go into the day-to-day fulfillment of

a life consecrated to God. The scope of this work focuses on the elements which make up the basis of religious life, the three vows and common life. Moving then to the necessity of a dynamic communication with God, Father explores the prophetic, apostolic and ecclesial dimensions of the closer "following of Christ." Basing himself as always on the conciliar and post-conciliar writings, Father Gambari achieves a complete picture of the religious in the present milieu.
266 pages; cloth $5.00; paper $4.00

The Updating of Religious Formation
Rev. Elio Gambari, SMM

Text and Commentary of the "Instruction on the Renewal of Religious Formation," Renovationis causam. Guidelines and principles; special norms and their application. Includes a comparative study of Canon Law and the Instruction.
150 pages; cloth $2.50; paper $1.50

Please order from addresses on following page.

Sisters,
    Please send me:

_____

_____

_____

_____

name _____

address_____

city _____ state _____ zip_____

Enclosed is my payment for $_____

Daughters of St. Paul

IN MASSACHUSETTS
    50 St. Paul's Avenue, Boston, Ma. 02130
    172 Tremont Street, Boston, Ma. 02111
IN NEW YORK
    78 Fort Place, Staten Island, N.Y. 10301
    59 East 43rd St., New York, N.Y. 10017
    625 East 187th Street, Bronx, N.Y. 10458
    525 Main Street, Buffalo, N.Y. 14203
IN NEW JERSEY
    84 Washington Street, Bloomfield, N.J. 07003
IN CONNECTICUT
    202 Fairfield Avenue, Bridgeport, Ct. 06603
IN OHIO
    2105 Ontario St. (at Prospect Ave.), Cleveland, Oh. 44115
    25 E. Eighth Street, Cincinnati, Oh. 45202
IN PENNSYLVANIA
    1719 Chestnut St., Philadelphia, Pa. 19103
IN FLORIDA
    2700 Biscayne Blvd., Miami, Fl. 33137
IN LOUISIANA
    4403 Veterans Memorial Blvd.,
      Metairie, La. 70002
    86 Bolton Avenue, Alexandria, La. 71301
IN MISSOURI
    1001 Pine St. (at North 10th), St. Louis, Mo. 63101
IN TEXAS
    114 East Main Plaza, San Antonio, Tx. 78205
IN CALIFORNIA
    1570 Fifth Avenue, San Diego, Ca. 92101
    278 17th Street, Oakland, Ca. 94612
    46 Geary Street, San Francisco, Ca. 94108
IN HAWAII
    1184 Bishop St., Honolulu, Hi. 96813
IN ALASKA
    750 West 5th Avenue
    Anchorage, Ak. 99501
IN CANADA
    3022 Dufferin Street, Toronto 395, Ontario, Canada
IN ENGLAND
    57, Kensington Church Street, London W. 8, England
IN AUSTRALIA
    58, Abbotsford Rd., Homebush, N.S.W., Sydney 2140,
    Australia